Praise for Jennifer Ackerman and *Notes from the Shore*

"In the tradition of Anne Morrow Lindbergh's *Gift from the Sea* or William Warner's *Beautiful Swimmers*, a book about life on and off the shore . . . a joy to read. The writing is elegant and the book is full of lovely images."
—*The Washington Post*

"Compassionate, soothing and wondrous, this elegant book will be admired, even loved, for as long as there is water and sky and land."
—Rick Bass

"Ackerman, blessed with a naturalist's eye for detail and a poet's soul, beautifully captures the ebb and flow of life at this edge of marsh, sand, and sea."
—*People*

"Ackerman writes enchantingly of an environment we all have experienced, but perhaps have never paused to 'see.' Through her eyes, and her remarkable skills of description, we share a world as complex and exciting as the unfathomable depths of the oceans."
—*The Baltimore Sun*

"This is the alchemy of art with solid science—the real thing. What a debut!"
—Edward Hoagland

"A book to dip into and to re-read; the chapter 'Between Tides' alone is worth the price of admission."
—Sue Hubbell

PENGUIN BOOKS

NOTES FROM THE SHORE

Jennifer Ackerman has written widely on natural history and the sciences. She has been a staff writer at the National Geographic Society, and her essays and articles have appeared in *The New York Times*, *Nature Conservancy*, and many other magazines and newspapers. She lives in Virginia with her husband, novelist Karl Ackerman, and their two daughters.

Notes

from

the

Shore

JENNIFER ACKERMAN

Illustrated by Karin Grosz

PENGUIN BOOKS

PENGUIN BOOKS
Published by the Penguin Group
Penguin Books USA Inc., 375 Hudson Street,
New York, New York 10014, U.S.A.
Penguin Books Ltd, 27 Wrights Lane, London W8 5TZ, England
Penguin Books Australia Ltd, Ringwood, Victoria, Australia
Penguin Books Canada Ltd, 10 Alcorn Avenue,
Toronto, Ontario, Canada M4V 3B2
Penguin Books (N.Z.) Ltd, 182–190 Wairau Road,
Auckland 10, New Zealand

Penguin Books Ltd, Registered Offices: Harmondsworth, Middlesex, England

First published in the United States of America by Viking Penguin,
a division of Penguin Books USA Inc., 1995
Published in Penguin Books 1996

3 5 7 9 10 8 6 4

THE LIBRARY OF CONGRESS HAS CATALOGUED THE HARDCOVER AS FOLLOWS:
Ackerman, Jennifer.
Notes from the shore/Jennifer Ackerman.
p. cm.
ISBN 0-670-84924-3 (hc.)
ISBN 0 14 01.7788 4 (pbk.)
1. Lewes (Del.)—Description and travel.   2. Natural history—Delaware—
Lewes.   3. Landscape—Delaware—Lewes.   I. Title.
F174.L6A25 1995
917.51'7—dc20   94–41254

Printed in the United States of America
Set in Weiss
Designed by Jo Metsch

For Karl and Zoë
and for my mother,
Kathryn Aring Morton

Contents

Exultation is the going
Of an inland soul to sea
—*Emily Dickinson*

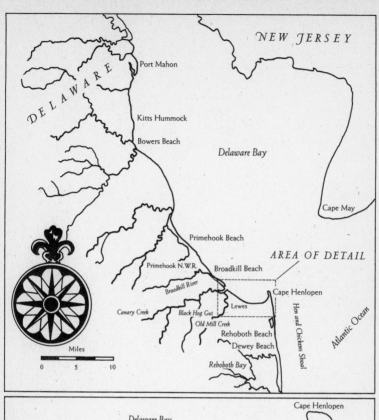

NEW JERSEY

DELAWARE

Port Mahon

Kitts Hummock

Bowers Beach

Delaware Bay

Cape May

Primehook Beach

AREA OF DETAIL

Primehook N.W.R.   Broadkill Beach

Broadkill River   Cape Henlopen

Canary Creek   *Black Hog Gut*   Lewes   *Hen and Chickens Shoal*

Old Mill Creek   *Atlantic Ocean*

Rehoboth Beach

Dewey Beach

Rehoboth Bay

Miles

0   5   10

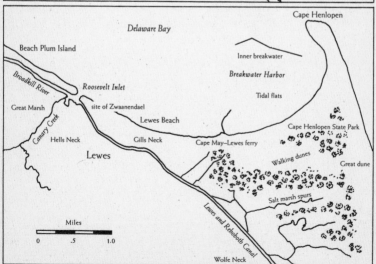

Cape Henlopen

Delaware Bay

Beach Plum Island

Inner breakwater

Broadkill River   *Breakwater Harbor*

Roosevelt Inlet   Tidal flats

Great Marsh   site of Zwaanendael

Lewes Beach   Cape Henlopen State Park

Canary Creek   Hells Neck   Gills Neck   Cape May–Lewes ferry

Lewes   *Walking dunes*   Great dune

Lewes and Rehoboth Canal   Salt marsh spurs

Wolfe Neck

Miles

0   .5   1.0

Delaware Bay (top); *Cape Henlopen and environs* (bottom)

Notes

from

the

Shore

Prologue

$\mathscr{I}$ live in a small town by the sea. It sits just inside Cape Henlopen at the bottom lip of the Delaware Bay. Summer mornings, salt air sifts through the screen on my open window. Companies of gulls settle on my rooftop or sail around the church steeple across the way. On gray days, the foghorn out in the harbor bleats like a cow deprived of its calf.

One is always aware of the sea in Lewes, can feel its broad, enduring presence just over the fat humps of sand dunes. It affects people as surely as it breeds rhythms into the fiddler crab. When the wind is from the east, the saltwater leans in strong, and the sun rises pink under a moist haze. Stamps mate shamelessly. Bread molds in a day. In big storms, the ocean seems to empty its belly, and even a solid house like mine feels ephemeral. The hackberry trees weep floods of tears; my drainspout gives up altogether, spewing a wide waterfall that feeds a pool at the foot of the stairs. In the small tidal marsh at the center of town, chill water rises to the tips of the cordgrass so that only specks of green show, like a lawn in a pointillist painting. When the tide shrinks, the mudbanks exhale that sharp, salty smell.

Some days, a thick sea mist creeps backward over the dunes and infiltrates the town with the ghost of deep water; then the place feels as if it were adrift, unanchored to anything.

This coast is a rhythmic landscape cut from marshes and sand and described by an early Dutchman as "beautifully level." Age by age the ocean has risen; age by age it falls again, sweeping back and forth across the coastal plain. The ground around Lewes supports flowering plants that fare well in thin sandy soil: beach heather, bayberry, groundsel, beach pea. Because the ocean tempers the swing of seasons, it is a twin province of north and south, home to species that ordinarily do not mix. Bald cypress, muscadine grape, loblolly pine, and sweetleaf push up from their southern habitats; wild cherry, beach plum, sassafras, and laurel creep down from the north. Such northern species as eider ducks meet true southerners like the brown pelican and black vulture.

Spring and fall, flocks of migrating birds flow north and south overhead. In May, shorebirds descend from night skies to feed on our margins. Swallows mass under the August sun, stippling the dunes and beading the phone wires. When the temperature falls, the air reverberates with the calls of snow geese, which gather by the thousand in the stubbly cornfields like raucous crowds on a public beach. In winter, flotillas of scoters and scaups play the edges of the sea.

The Siconese Indians called this spot Sickoneysinck, or "place where there is a gentle sound from the movement of things." Early Dutch colonists called it Zwaanendael for the wild swans. Today Lewes is a town of twenty-five hundred,

Cape Henlopen

though the population swells in summer. It has been spared the development that mars so much of this coast thanks in part to the clouds of mosquitoes that once bred in its marshes and ponds, and to the presence of two strong-smelling fish-fertilizer plants on its bay shore, which perfumed the streets, especially when the wind was from the east.

Our main thoroughfare, Savannah Road, got its name from the flat farmland over which it traveled. Some of this land remains, and roadside stands piled high with sweet white corn and cantaloupes still populate the county highways in summer. But with the death of the fish factories in the late sixties, Lewes has grown into nearby Wolfe Neck, Gills Neck, and Holland Glade, slapping down over forest and farmfield subdivisions with names that memorialize what has been razed.

At the only stoplight in town, Savannah intersects Pilot-town Road, which runs along the Lewes canal. This is the old neighborhood of the river pilots, men charged with navigating large vessels through the swift, narrow channel of the Delaware to ports upstream. When the wind is right, you can hear their boats go out, the throbbing engines louder than most other boats. The pilots are still considered the elite and their houses are among the biggest and best in town, with tall attic windows once used to scan the horizon for incoming ships. Maps of the Delaware Bay are peppered with reminders of the old terror of the cold, gray deeps: Ship John Shoal, Joe Flogger Shoal, Old Bare Shoal, Deadman Shoal, The Shears. The bay is a drowned river valley of modest size, about seventy-five miles north to south from its head at Chester, Pennsylvania, to its broad mouth at Cape Henlopen and Cape May. Unlike the Chesapeake Bay, its shoreline is not shredded by necks and coves but smooth and regular, like a beet. It receives a vigorous infusion of freshwater from the Delaware, the Schuylkill, and a dozen or so smaller rivers—the Neversink, Smyrna, Mispillion, Murderkill, Broadkill—which mixes at the mouth with saltwater from the sea. The floor of the bay is strewn with ships that have foundered over the past three centuries, casualties of the shoals that radiate fingerlike north and west from its mouth and sometimes rise nearly to the surface. Before the advent of the river pilots, it is said, the curbs of the town's sidewalks were built from the masts of wrecked vessels.

Most of the houses in Lewes are small, modest frame houses from the 1700s or large Victorian affairs built during the railroad boom of the late nineteenth century. The older ones have long sloping roofs, dormer windows, and cypress shingles hand-cut from virgin trees felled in the swamps near Laurel, Delaware, now weathered to a soft gray. They have that native sense of geometry and proportion, compatible in mood and color with the beach, the marsh, the sea. The Victorian places, on the other hand, stand out like big showpieces, fussy with scrollwork and ornately carved porches. The house I live in is one of these. My father and stepmother bought it twenty years ago, when it was an oversized, shabby elephant of a place, grayish white like dried salt. They fell in love with it largely because of the dozens of giant double-hung windows that admit sunlight from all sides. Over the years they fixed it up and slowly furnished it with odd pieces hand-picked from local estate sales. Then they generously offered up its three apartments to a tribe of relatives: brother, daughter, mother, two elderly aunts—the one quiet and polite, the other, voluble and brusque but with a big, generous spirit that still haunts the place, along with the stray cats she adopted. And finally, my husband and me, who came three years ago with the plan to start a family of our own here.

When I arrived, I set as my goal to look closely at the daily nature around me and by so doing, come to know the place a little. There is not a great deal on this coast that recalls the landscape of my childhood. My roots lie in the interior, in rolling deciduous woodland. Few of us have the privilege of living as adults in the place we lived in as children. Even fewer of us die where we were born. I have moved eight times in the last nine years. How many landscapes can fit inside the human heart?

At first I felt disoriented here, as if I had been spun round blindfolded and set down reeling, wondering from which quarter the wind usually blew and whether this shroudy brown fog was typical of my share of coast. I missed the hiss of wind in high trees and the sweet vegetable smell of humus and decay-

Beach grass with osprey feather

ing leaves. I saw only the barren mud flats, the sly sameness of the marsh. I saw only surfaces.

A native landscape enters a child's mind through a meld of sensations: the smell of seaweed or hay, the sound of cicadas, the cold grit of stone. It is all heart and magic, confusion rather than order, but the feeling it evokes is wholly satisfying and lasting. Gaining this kind of deep familiarity with a landscape other than your native one is like learning to speak a foreign language. You can't hope for quick or easy fluency. You work from the outside in, by accumulating a vocabulary of observed details. You learn where things happen in the rhythmic revolutions of the days and the year, which shrubs harbor families of grackles, which stands of beach plum send out sprays of August bloom, where the hognose snake waits for its toad and the toad, for its fly. Slowly the strange becomes familiar; the familiar becomes precious.

In my time here, I've learned that the slick dark mud flat is fidgety with hidden creatures, that life here is equally in the rapid pulse of perceptible change and in the slow pull of long time, that with a small nest egg of facts about a place comes a sea of questions. I've learned that the way in to a new land-scape is to pull at a single thread. Nearly always it will lead to the heart of the tangle.

Harbor

of

Refuge

The watchtower at Cape Henlopen rises seventy feet from the back slope of the great dune, a sand hill that for a hundred years or more has been moving southwestward like some great quartz whale. Inside the tower, it is cool and damp and echoes with reverberating footsteps on metal stairs. Viewing slats grid the walls with slanted bars of light. From the top platform, the view extends about ten miles.

Along the northeast edge of the bay runs a wide swath of forest. The trees are mainly pitch pine and loblolly. Beyond, the cape unfurls between the bay and sea, framed by two stone breakwaters. To the west is Spartina marsh, shot through with fingerlike ridges of pine, and beyond that, the roofs and steeples of Lewes; to the south lie sand dunes and an old salt pond. Peppering the dunes are concrete bunkers and more watchtowers built during World War II. The cape was made an army base in 1941, part of the Atlantic coastal defense network, a top-secret, heavily armed fort where two thousand soldiers and sailors kept watch for German spies and saboteurs. Now it is a park, and nature encroaches everywhere, softening the hard edges of military litter. Pavement bristles with grass. The trumpet vine planted *for camouflage has run wild over fences and debris. Sand seeps through the windows and doors of the old army buildings. At least one watchtower is a bubble off plumb, its base undermined by the shifting sand and rising tide.*

Seen from above, the land has the air of geographical simplicity, but it is full of subtle peaks and hollows, low wet swales stuffed with strange flora: the red-capped green lichen known as British soldier, the long runners of club moss growing in boggy depressions alongside cranberries, and spatulate-leaved sundew, a carnivorous plant that turns fly to carrion.

It is a gray day in February with no deep overcast but a cold haze. At the cape, a male redwing blackbird is forcing spring, announcing his territorial boundaries with a flash of wings and tail to tell fellow blackbirds that this thicket belongs to him. I like to botanize in winter, study the bark of naked trees, the dried husks of grasses and weeds. Aldo Leopold said that our plant biases are in part traditional. My maternal grandmother in long sleeves and a straw hat yanked the purple loosestrife that grew rank and alien in her midwestern garden—she called it "purple peril"—so I look askance at the plant despite its pretty bloom. I admire winter weeds because my mother did, the threadbare corset of Queen Anne's lace, the reeds starchy and whited. Plants wear their skeletons on the outside. In winter just this remains, their structural essence.

A red cedar stands before me on the sand like a buoy in a dune sea. *Juniperus virginiana*. It is full and vigorous, a female judging from its tiny blue berrylike cones, which even in this cold smell faintly of gin. Beneath its brown shreddy bark is beautiful heartwood, rose-red and durable. Its needlelike leaves are as rusty as an old fender. I've seen cedars four stories high, but this one barely makes eight feet, a far cry from the green flame of a van Gogh cypress. Here on the land's edge, trees rarely reach their full proportions, especially not those right up against the sea. Nearby pitch pines and loblollies are also clipped by the salt breeze, their crowns whittled into harmony with the contours of the rolling dunes, trunks gnarled and branches sweeping low to the ground. It is hard to understand how they thrive at all with the heavy load of shifting sand and withering doses of sodium chloride. But these junipers are tough old conifers, descended from that ancient group of cone-bearing plants that appeared sometime in the late Carboniferous period, about three hundred million years ago. They now grow on the solid upper rock of the Himalayas to twelve thousand feet and here, a few yardsticks above the sea.

It was among these cedars and pines that I surprised a hognose snake. Squatting on my heels in a bright patch of sun one spring morning, I saw a stocky yellow-brown snake patterned with dark blotches emerge from a thicket and shoot across the sandy floor. I went after it and cornered it at the roots of a pine tree. *Heterodon platyrhinos*, thick-bodied and harmless, but with the ghastly habit of swallowing toads live. It gathered in a coil, puffed up its neck, and hissed with ferocity. I held my ground. It hissed again, lunged forward, and hissed some more, but this time with less enthusiasm, then slithered away into the brush. The hognose puts on a good show. If I had persisted, it might have struck once or twice, then tried a different tack, flopping over on its back, mouth agape, lolling its tongue in perfect semblance of death.

An ice-wind is cutting to the bone. Across the dunes, the tide has laid up sheets of ice in stratified shelves along the shore. I sink my fists deep into my pockets and bury my chin in my chest. I try to make a point of venturing out in all weathers,

Winter at Cape Henlopen

even if only to feel for a moment the energies of the outside world. The habit began in my twenty-first year. In that year my mother died. She was a woman well loved, strong, self-sacrificing, in her early years a scholar of Melville and Gerard Manley Hopkins and, later, a passionate defender of the rights of the retarded and the mainstay of our large, splintered family. News of her illness reached me at school in Connecticut. It came in her exhausted voice in spring, months past the date of diagnosis. Cancer of the cervix, treatments underway. The day I went to see her in the hospital, the March sky was clear blue and free of weathers. The trees had just begun to leaf out. No flowers, she had said, so I searched the roadsides for dried weeds to bundle into a lasting bouquet, but everything was nipped in shoots of raw green, committed to spring.

We spent the month of May at home together, sitting for hours on the brick patio behind the house, she stretched out on a plastic lawn chair and I squatting on my heels, painting an old wrought-iron bench that had been in the family for years. We talked hesitantly about who would care for Beckie, my profoundly retarded little sister, but resolved nothing. It was too complicated, too painful. My mom had devoted much of her own life to buttressing Beckie's. She didn't want to burden me; I didn't want to make promises I wouldn't keep. Mostly we talked about little things. When I think back on our closeness, it had always been forged of these: a shared love of old wooden objects, of chocolate bars and sweet pickles and cheese, of memorizing poetry, making chili, having our hair combed by other hands. As we talked, my painting progressed slowly, partly because I wanted to draw out the project, make it last—it was good to have something to do with my hands—and partly because of a steady stream of black ants that for some mysterious reason were drawn to the wet paint, stuck tight, and smothered there despite my efforts at rescue.

By June my mother had worsened and was back in the hospital. In July she came home to die. The doctors told her it would be a quick end, quicker if she refused food and water. She did, for ten days—her powerful mothering hands cold despite the heat, her lips dry and cracked—held back from death only by a splendid heart that would not let go.

Proust wrote of his mother's death that he felt like a butterfly breaking its chrysalis to assume mature form. I felt the vulnerability of metamorphosis, but never the butterfly. Part of my life had been sheared away by my mother's going, that huge part I had supposed established and safe. My grief was endless and awkward, welling up and spilling over, making my mind whirl in small, dark circles. That winter, I found a secluded spot an hour from my home in New Haven, a small mountain with a path up the backside that opened at the top to a magnificent view of a horseshoe meander in a river. I visited the place regularly through the seasons, let its little details sink in, the trail carpeted with pine needles, the rotting logs with their bloom of fungus, the moss-covered rocks. I found comfort in the innumerable small but important events going on, things coming to their own place in a regular way, resilient, persistent. I discovered in nature the same appeal I found in books. Both were engrossing, filled with the richness of particularities and yet mysteriously universal. Both were the stuff of perspective. *noticing*

The thicket of shrubs and vines hedging this stunted forest holds winged sumac with a drooping fist of hairy red seeds, good for birds in a winter pinch. Also, greenbrier, oddly enough a member of the lily family. Despite its tiny hooked snags it is popular among deer as browse and among rabbits as shelter. The few remaining leaves on the bayberry and wax myrtle are as aromatic as ever, with the sweet fragrance of spice.

What else? Vines of summer grape, still sporting clutches of dark purple berries, the tough dried black husks of earthstars, twists of poverty grass, panicum, and switchgrass, and a singular plant: *Yucca filamentosa*, a rosette of spiky green leaves, each frayed with curly threads. From the yucca's nest of swords rises a single woody stalk that bears upturned cuplike seed capsules, winter mockeries of the creamy bell-shaped flowers that bloom in June.

A stand of prickly pear has apparently punched the clock for winter; its pads are bruised and broken, splayed flat against the sand. It will swell in spring, inflate like a balloon, and send out a brilliant yellow flower that draws the praise of bees. It has no showy spines, but fine tufts of tiny barbed bristles that slip beneath the skin and cause great irritation.

"To understand plants," writes botanist E. J. H. Corner, "it is necessary to think right back into their most unfamiliar beginnings." For the prickly pear and the cedar, the baobab and sapodilla, those beginnings lie in the sea. The first microscopic plant cells evolved in the gray salt waters. Not in the abyssal depths, but in the sunlit, element-rich shoals above the continental shelf. On a warm damp margin of some early body of water, the first roots held fast, then spread wandering fingers of green over an earth raw and untouched by life. Those plants that colonized the land retained the principles of construction and growth born in the water. But moving to land required two things: waterproofing their simple stems and providing strength so they could stand upright. "Land plants are understood as seaweeds," writes Corner, "dried off on the surface, waxed against evaporation, rooted, piped for water flow, built up with the transparent bricks made from the excess of sugars."

A low matty plant spreads over the open dunes. Local people call it heather. Its botanical name is *Hudsonia tomentosa* and it falls into the unlovely category of subshrub. The great botanist Thomas Nuttall first described it when he came to the cape in June of 1809. He had left England the year before at the age of twenty-one to pursue an "ardent attachment" to botany. At the cape, he hoped to see a showy little vine called coral honeysuckle. But after carefully searching the place, he couldn't find it. "It had either been taken up to supply gardens," he wrote, "or has been buried in the advancing and almost perpendicular sand hills, which skirt the wood on the side next to the sea." He found instead a plant new to science and full of fine yellow blossom. He called it *Hudsonia* after the Henry who had discovered this cape exactly two hundred years earlier, and *tomentosa* for its tough, needlelike leaves. These leaves are enmeshed with a thick coat of whitish hairs that hold in moisture and protect the plant from the dunes' heat, which can reach 125 degrees. *Hudsonia* thrives in migrating dunes; its capacity to trap sand slows the creeping movement.

In the early morning before the wind rises, I find these dunes scribed with the comings and goings of snakes, voles, and pine lizards. Here on a sunbaked slope is the pit of a creature with a name like an oxymoron or an odd chimera out of my childhood bestiary: the ant lion. It is the larva of a delicate, long-bodied insect. In its adult form, the creature looks like a damselfly, but its larva is a grotesque, wedge-shaped thing the color of slate with long, bristling sicklelike jaws. It digs a conical pit by moving backward in a circle, plowing the sand with the tip of its sharp abdomen and flipping the grains upwards with its flat head. The pit is about the width of a child's thumb and perfectly engineered as a live trap. The smooth, sloping sides form an angle of exactly 32 degrees, the angle of repose for sand grains. The ant lion lies in wait at the apex of the pit, all but its jaws concealed. When an ant stumbles over the edge, it starts an avalanche of sand on the slipface, loses its toehold, and tumbles into the jaws of the larva. With a quick jab, the ant lion pierces its prey, sucks out the juices, and then flips the empty body out of the trap.

Fringing the dunes is straw-colored beach grass. Slender in construction, its spikelet set on a fine stock, it doesn't lean hard against the wind, but bends and sways, scribing tiny arcs in the sand. It is practical as well as pretty. When I look through a hand lens, I can see the parallel ridges of its leaves. In the hollows between the ridges are the tiny air pores necessary for photosynthesis. When conditions get too dry, the blades roll inward, sealing the pores. The plant's genius includes an elaborate underground stratagem. Its long searching root network extends impressively to seek moisture at lonely depths, down to forty feet. Then the roots branch profusely. Once established, the plant relies little on the vagaries of wind or animal to spread to new ground, but sends out rhizomes, or horizontal stems, that run a few inches under the surface. Each spring, the rhizomes produce staunch new shoots. Even so slight an obstruction as a thin new shoot makes the wind drop its load, and a tiny triangular shadow of sand builds up behind the plant. The beach grass pumps out more roots and stems, roots and stems, knitting together the growing dune like sod.

On a winter afternoon near twilight, waves are coursing in from the northeast, rearing up and pouring down with a wild, pitching crash. They are plunging breakers, the kind of wave whose crest moves faster than its body, creating a smooth, glassy hollow, a tunnel in the water. The spilling breaker—a wave that breaks slowly, its crest sliding down its forward side—is rare here, and surging waves, those that move up the beach without breaking, are unheard of. Such tidy taxonomical categories give the impression of uniformity, but each wave is unique, born of intricate combinations of breezes, planetary gyres, and tiny puffs gathered over the sea. I've read that you can tell the origin of a wave from its shape and behavior. Waves formed recently by strong offshore winds have a peaked shape and spill scuds of foam down their steep slopes as they approach, then break gradually and deliberately. Those that have traveled long distances rear up in the surf zone, curl forward, and crash suddenly into their troughs.

These plungers were probably born of a squall somewhere in the distant sea, collecting force from the winds and transporting it patiently across thousands of miles. I know that a wave is no solid body, but a pattern of energy that briefly molds the water as it passes, Conrad's "swath of silk undulating in the breeze." Still, these waves, coming as they do all the way from some distant part of the north Atlantic to sprawl flat on this sandbar, impress me. They are messengers from another time and place, like starlight.

I've always loved the language of the sea. Sitting in classes on oceanography, I found myself transported willy-nilly by its vocabulary. There were swells, those long, low undulations arising from waves that have traveled beyond the wind system that generated them. As a swell approaches shore, it "feels bottom." There was fathom, from the Old English word for outstretched arms. Said Joyce, after Shakespeare: "Five fathoms out there. Full fathom five thy father lies. At one he said. Found drowned." There was the deep-scattering layer, the concentration of huge numbers of crustaceans, fish, and other small organisms that migrate vertically in the water column, up during the night and down during the day. There was the neap tide and the spring tide, the latter having nothing to do with seasons, of course, but with the time of year when the moon, earth, and sun line up in a syzygy, and the moon's gravity, combined with the sun's, tugs on Earth's moonside waters and on the opposite side as well, causing the tides to spring up higher over the land. (The spring tide was loved by shipbuilders, writes Samuel Eliot Morison, because it enabled them to build their vessels at convenient places at the head of the tidewater, in their backyards, if they wished, and launch them at the top of the spring ebb.) Reading Melville or Conrad, my mind would wander at the mention of such nautical terms as dead reckoning, the calculating of a ship's position by distances covered and course steered. Or sleek, defined by Melville as "the smooth, satin-like surface produced by the subtle moisture thrown off by the whale." The language of the sea-floor was nothing if not metaphorical. The zone of darkness below a hundred fathoms was the bathyal, from the Greek for deep; below a thousand fathoms was the abyssal, from the Latin *abyssus*, or bottomless gulf; and below thirty-five hundred fathoms, the hadal, from the French for hell.

The effort to stratify the sea, to name and categorize waves—"to unpack the huddling and gnarls of the water and law out the shapes and the sequence of the running," in Gerard Manley Hopkins's words—is part of the effort to get a handle on the chaos of the sea, bring it under the net of human language. I still take deep pleasure in this vocabulary and am delighted to live in a place where daily life requires its use.

This coast faces slightly north of east, so the waves come in at an angle, creating a current that flows parallel to the beach just offshore. This longshore current scours sand from beaches to the south and carries it in a zigzag sawtooth stream northward—an aberration on the mid-Atlantic coast, where the net drift is southerly. In a year, half a million cubic yards of sand move past this place, enough to fill several thousand dump trucks. That's a respectable flow—midway between the ten thousand cubic yards that flow west along Waikiki Beach and the million that sail south past Santa Monica—most of it stolen from the resorts of Rehoboth, Dewey Beach, and Bethany Beach and deposited at the tip of Cape Henlopen.

On the ocean side of the cape at winter low tide or after a severe storm has scoured the beach, there emerges from the surf the stumps of an old cedar forest. Tiny crystals of sand have slowly cut away the trees' outer growth and left only heartwood.

The stumps rise from the sand like inselberge, like the buttes and peaks of Monument Valley. Scoured smooth and shiny, some are as sharp as an awl, some tangled with seaweed or stray fishing nets. They are all that is left of the cedar forest that Thomas Nuttall explored, long ago covered by sand.

At the edge of the forest there once stood a lighthouse, built in 1765 at the bidding of Philadelphia merchants who were losing ships to the shoals of the bay. It was seven stories of granite, situated amid cedars and pines on a high dune a quarter of a mile from the sea. In 1788 a committee of wardens charged with the maintenance of the lighthouse noted with some alarm the shifty nature of the site. They wrote to Benjamin Franklin, then president of the commonwealth of Pennsylvania:

> The land in the environs of this building [we] observe to be so changeable from strong currents of wind that within these few years, where there have been deep ponds, there are now moles considerably high; and on the contrary where there were hills of sand, there are now cale and hollows; every precaution should therefore be taken to secure the foundation from the growing effect of this evil.

In 1800 the keeper of the lighthouse first noticed the changing topography of the coast, the gradual northward movement of the cape's sands and the westward movement of the sea. By 1883, high waters lapped at the base of the dune on which the lighthouse sat. That year the barkentine *Minnie Hunter* stranded on a sandbar five hundred feet north of the lighthouse, temporarily halting erosion. Taking its cue from the beached ship, the Lighthouse Board ordered brush and stone jetties installed, but the tides swept them away as fast as they were laid. By the fall of 1924, it was clear that the tower was

The cape's walking dunes

doomed, and the Bureau of Lighthouses discontinued the light. After a severe storm in the spring of 1926 undermined the base of the lighthouse, a strong northeasterly wind knocked it down. Today its foundation lies a quarter of a mile out to sea.

Heraclitus said that you never step in the same stream twice. The coastal version of that is never walking the same shore twice. If I had to describe this place in three words, I would choose these: Nothing stays put. Every inch moves, shaped and reshaped by wind, waves, tides, and currents, not just on a daily but on a seasonal basis. If you could sit stock still and watch with a remembering eye, the forms of the beach would become momentary shapes like the shifting flames of a fire. The changes brought about by tide, storm, and season would ripple over the coast, dunes rising and falling, the broad floor of the intertidal beach expanding and contracting, shapes wavering and blowing, dying and being reborn, not in devastation but in constant rearrangement.

One day a few years ago, I was walking on a rocky path beside a river in late winter. The river was frozen solid, but the day had warmed enough to make me shed my coat and to melt the ice collected in the crevices of rocks. A noise like a rifle shot rang out, and the ice on the river shuddered. More explosions and long, low grumbles as the ice floe began to crack and heave, then collapsed in on itself and shot forward on the free flow of water. The event had probably been in the making for days, as sun and warm temperatures melted the edges of the floe and expanded tiny cracks and fissures. But like the fall of a tree, the result took place in a single noisy instant. Such transformations in the physical world happen all the time, but the change is either too slow for us to notice—visible only in an abstract sense, by scrutiny through eons—or too quick, taking place behind our backs, and we have only before-and-after pictures to prove that it occurred at all.

Not so at the shore. The sculpting often takes place right before our eyes. Waves roll in one by one, every five seconds or so. That's about 14,400 waves per day moving in to meet and reform the shore. The ocean takes away, it gives. Rarely in its natural state does the overall area of beach change. Sand removed is replaced in cyclic fashion. The shore is no dumb, immovable thing, but has a life and a wisdom of its own. In big storms, a great mass of sand disappears from the beach, dragged by waves out to sea, where it collects on offshore sandbars. These act as a break for the high, steep plungers that follow closely one upon the other. What is left is a meager strip of coarse, heavy, porous sand which can absorb those beating blue tons that would destroy concrete in just a few seasons.

Something similar happens in winter. One frigid morning I went down to the ocean to walk. As usual, I migrated to the water's edge seeking firm tread, but instead found myself caught in something like quicksand, sinking rapidly up to my calves, my knees, my thighs, before I finally managed to flop forward and extract myself, heart thumping, from the gritty soup. It was a tactile lesson in seasonal change on the shore, the transfer of fine sand from the swash zone, where it makes for firm walking, to offshore sandbars, where it acts as a break for winter storm waves. At home I pulled tiny seashells from the bottom of my socks.

Not long after I arrived here a story appeared in the local paper. A farmer named Wayne Aydelotte had been plowing a field just north of Lewes when he felt his plow strike something hard. He made a pass back and saw that it was the tip of a rock. It took three hours, three men, and a Massey Ferguson six-plow tractor to pull the boulder from its resting place. It measured six feet long, three feet wide, and three feet high, and weighed in at around four thousand pounds. Water from a rainy spring may have brought it to the surface, said one geologist, but more likely the rain had simply eroded the soil around it.

All great stones found here are migrants brought down from the north by glacier-swollen waters. No rumpled granite crops up in our lawns or bursts through the sandy soils of our pine forests. The old crystalline Piedmont rock below us is covered by a wedge of soft, unconsolidated marine sediments—

gravel, sand, and mud—eight thousand feet thick. Go down into the dark of time and you see that this wasn't always the case. Rocks as high as the Himalayas had their stint in the sun here. The domes of the ancestral Appalachians reached upwards of fifteen thousand feet. That was at the end of the Permian era, around 250 million years ago, near the time when the land-masses that are now Europe and Africa closed out the ocean and fused into that gigantic mass Pangaea, which held all of Earth's land within a single shore. Over the next hundred million years or so, the Atlantic opened up again as a puddle that grew. (It is still growing; each year the journey between New York and London takes a fraction of a second longer.) The ancestral Appalachians went from fractured white vertebrae to flat sandy expanse. This land has had an on-again-off-again history, now plain, now mountain, now plain. The last rise of mountains produced the modern Appalachians. Even as they heaved up, they were cut down by wind and rain. The detritus rolled onto the coastal plain and out onto the continental shelf, which accepted layer upon layer of heavy sediment until it sank from the weight.

For the last few million years, this region's deep geology has been fairly stable, but not its edges. These have moved east, then west, then east again as the sea has risen and fallen, sweeping back and forth across the coastal plain with the freezing and melting of glaciers. The effect has been to flatten things out and to create a coastline that is no line at all, but a kind of roaming, evanescent merge. It is pure chance that it lies in its present position.

One blowy March day, I joined a group planting beach grass on the dunes of Broadkill Beach and Beach Plum Island, northwest of Lewes. It was part of a larger effort, extending down to Dewey in the south, and involving the labor of an

eclectic bunch: girl scouts, boy scouts, hairdressers, shopkeep-
ers, students from the Epworth Christian School and Cape
Henlopen High, state bureaucrats, the Mobile Surf Fisherman's
Association, and the Four Seasons Motorcycle Club. We worked
in pairs, one member digging a hole, the other wedging in a
clump of strawlike grass before the hole collapsed in sand. I
worked by the side of a man who owns a house between
Broadkill Beach and the island. My work was casual, an interest
in the plant and the structure of the dune; his was urgent, an
effort to save the ground beneath his home. Near the center of
Broadkill Beach is a cottage on stilts that stood on dry land ten
years ago. Today, its long flamingo legs perch above water
fifty feet into the estuary.

The newspapers tell me that the land around Lewes is
considered among the best defended in the nation, under
steady surveillance by seven separate forces of law and order,
among them the Delaware River and Bay Authority, state,
town, and park police, and the United States Air Force, which
daily sends fighter jets overhead. But no one can stop what
people here see as the real thievery. Over the past century
most of the Delaware shore has been disappearing at an average rate of one to nine feet per year. Between 1850 and 1930,
Bethany lost three hundred feet of beach. In the early part of
this century, Port Mahon, farther north along the shore of the
estuary, retreated nearly twenty feet a year.

Beaches once went where they pleased. "There rolls the
deep where grew the tree," wrote Alfred, Lord Tennyson. Now
we try to bully them into proper conduct. Planting beach grass
at Beach Plum Island to stem the powerful marine pilferage is a
tame effort compared with the draconian steps taken elsewhere. At Port Mahon, a seawall of steel and timber keeps the
shore in place. At Pickering Beach, just to its south, scrap tires

act as floating breakwaters to cut the erosive force of waves. Kitts Hummock has fixed breakwaters built of stone, sand-filled nylon bags, and precast concrete boxes, a demonstration project courtesy of the Army Corps of Engineers. South of Lewes, at Ocean City, Maryland, a groin field keeps a wide berth of white sand in front of the big resort hotels, but only by starving another beach downstream. These groins have robbed the sandy expanse of Assateague Island, accelerating erosion from two feet a year to thirty-six. In the last half century, the northern two miles of Assateague nearest Ocean City has somersaulted over itself. Now the island has no place to go. Within twenty or thirty years it will likely disappear.

The Army Corps of Engineers once proposed a solution to the problem of erosion on this coast: an offshore breakwater stretching from Ocean City to Cape Henlopen, made of sunken surplus World War II cargo vessels. Fortunately the enterprise proved too expensive. It was not an original idea: A sixteenth-century Dutch dikemaster recommended sinking old ships and dumping earth on top of them to make artificial islands. But he also warned, "Water will not be compelled by any fortse, or it will return that fortse onto you."

We humans may have evolved in grasslands, but of late we have spun out from the prairie center and landed on the periphery. People move to the littoral like moths to a porchlight. "Nothing will content them but the extremest limit of the land," wrote Melville. What is the draw of the edge? When I come to face the sea, the great bulk of the land at my back falls away. It is the measurable and the known; before me is all unfathomed magnitude and mystery. If there is magic on this planet, it lies beneath that azure surface. "Surely the sea is the most beautiful fact in our universe," says poet Mary Oliver. "The sea is as near as we come to another world," says Anne Stevenson. And Derek Walcott: "The sea is History." For people like me who measure their land in square feet, not acres, who have lost the rhythm of harvest, the surge and drain of tides threads the day, gives the place a kind of meter, as in poetry. The sea is Conrad's accomplice of human restlessness. Its briny surf and shifting sand correspond to a memory as deep as any we possess. Solid as we seem, we are liquid beings, three-quarters water like the planet, and composed of motion down to the agitated atoms in our cells. Perhaps this is why we like to sleep where the thunder-suck of waves fills the night.

On the wall of my study is a map of the seacoast of Maryland, Delaware, and Virginia as it appeared around 1690. The map is roughly drawn and some of its features are a little fanciful, but the topography of the coastline is rendered fairly accurately. The map shows Cape Henlopen as a smooth, blunt knuckle of land bending 90 degrees where the sea turns into the bay. In the last three centuries, the cape has shifted north, narrowed, sprouted a thumb of land, lengthened, moved north and then west and then north again to assume its present long-fingered shape.

In 1831 William Strickland drew the first geologically precise map of the cape's topography and geomorphic features. An architect and engineer, Strickland was hired to oversee the biggest U.S. government engineering project ever attempted, the Delaware Breakwater. The Congress had authorized the building of the breakwater in response to a petition by merchants of Philadelphia and Wilmington. As river pilots know, the best approach to the Delaware River is a narrow tidal channel sixty to ninety feet deep that runs close to the Delaware shore. For years, shipping had concentrated here—and so had disaster. Between 1821 and 1825, merchants reported two hundred cases of shipwreck and loss. In squally weather, a lighthouse simply wasn't enough. The merchants wanted a shelter for their vessels, a harbor of refuge.

The first stones were sailed down to Lewes from Palisades-on-the-Hudson in 1829 and dropped into the six-fathom waters of the bay. Built solely with sailpower and sweat, the project spanned the terms of twelve presidents and cost more than $2 million. Roughly 2,500 feet long, with a 1,400-foot ice breaker, it was considered a marvel of engineering, the largest such structure in the western hemisphere and second in size only to the breakwater in Plymouth, England.

Seeking firewood and building material, workmen installing the breakwater harvested cedars, pines, and other vegetation from the cape shore. Northwest winds lifted the stripped sand into a great dune. Measurements taken during the Civil War showed that this great sand hill was moving southwestward at the rate of eleven feet a year, erasing the weeds and shrubs of a mature back-barrier forest, erasing at last the trees themselves, until the forest was only a swelling of sand eighty-five feet high.

There were other changes, too. When Strickland drew his map, the projected harbor created by the breakwater was deep and wide, with good access to the open ocean. But the engineer noted that the stone structure, though still in its infancy, had changed the direction and speed of currents along the shoreline. The river of sand that had moved smoothly around the blunt nose of the cape was deflected and dropped its load. The harbor had started to shoal.

Thirteen years after construction of the breakwater began—long before it was finished—Lewes Harbor was already too shallow for vessels of the largest class. By 1910, it had received such a massive dose of sediment that it showed a depth of less than twelve feet and was useless to all but the smallest ships. A new breakwater was started that year, sixty-five hundred feet north of the old one, designed to create a new harbor that would accommodate ships with deep drafts.

Meanwhile, the cape had begun to change shape. Fed by sand carried in the new pattern of currents, it grew north and west thirty to forty feet each year. As it migrated out toward the breakwater, the new fingerlike spit cut off the sand that once flowed in longshore currents around the old curve of the cape to feed Lewes Beach, Broadkill Beach, Primehook Beach, and points north.

These days the cape grows as much as a hundred feet a year. At low tide, I walk over parts of the old harbor that were once submerged in fifty feet of water. Sometime in the next few decades, if no one interferes, the cape will arc around the inner breakwater, swallow it up, and revert to its former blunt cuspate shape. And as the floor of the harbor emerges, all muck and ooze, plants will root in the mud flats, gain a soggy foothold, and gradually creep up in dripping strands to colonize the new land.

$\mathcal{O}$*sprey*

The temperature this morning is 82 degrees. The relative humidity is 85 percent. The wind is all by the sea; here in the bay it is quiet and warm. I've come to the cape in the hopes of seeing a pair of osprey, newly mated and nesting on a wooden platform by the bay. But the birds are nowhere in sight. Instead I spot a photographer in a three-piece suit, and his subjects, a groom in tails and a bride in a starchy white, high-necked gown. It is a pretty scene: Behind the pair, dunes stretch to the sea, patchy mats of beach heather exploding with the yellow bloom of May. But the bride seems annoyed. Her satin pumps fight the avalanching dunes, heels probing the sand like the bill of a willet. She reaches out to the groom to steady herself, removes a shoe, and empties a long stream of grit. She looks young, barely twenty. Beads of sweat soak the lace rimming her veil. The flies are up; the warm air carries the stench of creatures rotting on the flats.

Yesterday I was lucky enough to catch the

ospreys copulating. Through my scope I could see the female in intimate detail perched on the edge of the platform, her glistening yellow eyes, the dusky shafts of her breastband, the soft green-gray of her feet. Her mate circled above, white belly shining in the sun. He whistled piercing notes, then dropped suddenly, dipping below the platform and swooping up to hover directly above her. He settled on her back gently, barely touching her with clenched talons, flapping his wings for balance. She tipped forward slightly, raising her tail high to the side to receive him. I watched, a little ashamed of my magnified view. They coupled in silence for twenty or thirty seconds. Then the female, with a light flutter of wings, shrugged off her mate, who slowly banked upward and slipped sidewise across the sky.

The osprey leapt into my heart from my first days here. For one thing, the big bird is easy to identify. So many shorebirds are what ornithologists call "LBJs," little brown jobs. These I tried to pin down in my notes with some vague hope of identifying them later. But the osprey's size, its white belly and dark carpal patches, its wings kinked at the wrist, gave it away. So did its slow whistled call, a penetrating *kyew, kyew,* which drifts down from overhead. I occasionally mistook a high-flying osprey for a gull, but eventually learned to read its pattern of flight: shallow wingbeats interspersed with long glides. Its movement was more purposeful and deliberate than a gull's, less flighty. The osprey's huge nests, most of them in open, public places, and its showy method of hunting—a dazzling power dive ending in a burst of spray—made it a conspicuous neighbor, familiar and expected.

When I was seven or eight I went bird-watching with my father from time to time. I remember rising before dawn reluctantly and heading out, stiff, sleepy, my shoes damp with dew. In a family of five girls, time alone with my dad was a rare pleasure, not to be missed. The two of us would feel our way along the towpath between the C & O Canal and the Potomac River, cool breeze on the backs of our necks, companionable in late starlight. We moved quietly, all eyes for the small woodland birds we hoped to spy from a distance. It would begin with one bird, maybe two, chipping away at the dark. Then the clear whistled note of a cardinal would rise and the trilling of a wood thrush, and the songs would pass from one bird to another, their swelling sounds lifting me up by my ears. As the stars faded and branches emerged against the sky, sudden small shapes would appear and disappear, fluttering and darting about, flashing between the leaves: sparrows, finches, warblers, which I could just barely make out in the darkness. I didn't try to identify them. At that hour the world was theirs. On the ride home in the car, I would sift through my father's well-thumbed volume of Roger Tory Peterson's *Field Guide to North American Birds*, neatly indexed with plastic tabs marking the division of families: *Paridae* (titmice), *Sittidae* (nuthatches), *Troglodytidae* (wrens), and *Parulidae* (wood warblers). I was a pushover for the neat little manual, a fine tool for thinking about diversity and order in the world.

What birds I saw on those excursions were mostly woodland species. When it came to shorebirds I was utterly lost. Some species were easy to pin down. The ruddy turnstone, for instance—a squat, aggressive little bird with a harlequin mask—or the black-bellied plover, with its long, elegant black bib. But the sandpipers were a different story. Peterson calls the littlest ones "peeps," the white-rumped, the semipalmated, the least. There are rules, of course—the least is the smallest, its diminutive size earning it the species name *minutilla*; the semipalmated has a shorter, stouter bill—but judging either bill or body size at a distance seemed hopeless. Then there was the matter of plumage, which changes from season to season like foliage and which differs from male to female, from juvenile to immature to adult. Same bird, different disguises. No sooner had I nailed down the various appearances of one migratory species than another had taken its place. It's no wonder Aristotle came up with the theory of transmutation: Birds change species with the seasons, he said. Redstarts, common in Greece throughout the summer, became robins in winter; summer garden warblers changed into winter black caps. He claimed to have seen the birds midway in their metamorphoses. Anyone who has tried to identify fall birds in their shabby molting plumage can understand the mistake.

I eventually found a tutor in Bill Frech, a kind, owlish man, now eighty, who has been a devoted observer of winged things since he was twelve. Bill is up and away every morning at dawn to make his rounds in a VW with a scope mounted on the window. Though he claims not to have any special knowledge of winds or weather, he knows where the birds will be on any particular day, where heavy rains form pools of standing water that draw glossy ibises and egrets, which hayfields have been cut over recently, making good habitat for golden plovers, which buoys offer refuge to storm petrels in heavy wind. He sees what he sees, he says, and a good part of his pleasure is in the chanciness of the enterprise. One morning might yield nothing more interesting than a common goldeneye or an upland plover, while the next turns up a stray swallow-tailed kite hovering over the Lewes water tower, an Australian silver gull, or two thousand gannets riding out a storm behind Hen and Chickens Shoal.

Bill sees the world of light and motion not in a continuum, he says, but in frozen frames, a series of discernible stop-watch tableaux, which helps him spot his quarry. He scours the edges of the land, the broad sweep of sky and sea, one section at a time, and nearly always turns up a bird. I have tried to learn to do this, to look for spots of stillness on the tossing sea, for movement among the stubble of a cut field, but I often miss the mark and must have my eye directed. Bill carries no field guides. He depends less on fieldmarks to identify a bird than on its jizz, a term that comes from the fighter pilot's acronym GIS for General Impression and Shape. He has taught me to recognize a semipalmated plover or to distinguish a yellowlegs from a willet without quite knowing how I do so, just as one recognizes a friend from a distance not by individual characteristics, but by shape and gait. Most sandpipers walk and probe, while the plover runs and pecks, runs and pecks. Spotted sandpipers teeter. The Maliseet Indians of Maine understood this. They called the bird *nan a-mik-tcus*, or "rocks its rump." The sanderling flies steadily along; the plover's flight is wilder, full of tilting twists and turns. Most warblers dart through trees, but myrtle warblers drift. Knowing the jizz of a bird is especially useful when it comes to identifying high-flying species: Canada geese flap constantly; cormorants glide, long black necks in eternal pursuit of tiny tufted heads; gannets dip like goldfinches; pelicans alternate flaps with a short sail. As Bill filled my head with these rules of thumb, the species slowly separated and gained names.

I have the good fortune to live within a three-mile radius of five active osprey nests. One sits atop a platform on the double cross-arms of an old utility pole in the marsh at the center of town, hard by a railroad and King's Highway. The highway

Ospreys

carries the crush of traffic disgorged from the Cape May–Lewes ferry, a steady stream of tourists hell-bent for a seaward peep. Another nest occupies a channel marker, a fancy site complete with a flashing red light powered by a solar panel and two bright orange warning signs. The rest sit on duckblinds and man-made platforms. The ospreys seem unbothered by all the human activity surrounding these sites. They are adaptable, versatile sorts, with a predilection for human ruins. An unkempt chimney, a vacant house, or a pile of fence rails gone back to nature draws them in. On an island in the Chesapeake Bay that was once a bombing range, ospreys nest on the busted-up car bodies used as targets. One pair set up housekeeping on the surface of an unexploded thousand-pound bomb.

Every year, within a day or two of St. Patrick's Day, as schooling fish move into the sun-warmed waters of the bay, the ospreys arrive on the south wind for the breeding season.

They fly in high and circle overhead, greeting each mudbank, each twist of creek with a high, clear whistle. Invariably a notice appears in the local paper: "The fish-hawk, Delaware's harbinger of spring, has finally arrived."

The spectacle of courtship follows soon after. The young male selects a nesting site and then begins an aerial display, a slow, undulating flight high in the sky. Once an understanding is struck between a male of good property and his discriminating partner, nest building begins. The pair is up and down, in and out all day, scouring the neighborhood for appropriate materials. Ospreys are pack rats and indefatigable renovators. Though they nest in the same site from year to year, the nests themselves are often destroyed between seasons and so need considerable repairs. The birds don't seem particularly interested in permanence or stability. John Muir purportedly rode out a hurricane sitting on an eagle's nest. Ornithologist Alan Poole said he wouldn't trust his weight to an osprey nest on a blue windless day. At the nest near King's Highway, I've watched males bring in cornstalks, cow dung, crab shells, a fertilizer bag, a toy shovel, a slice of floor mat, and the doilylike remnants of fish net. Even this eclectic nest doesn't hold a candle to one John Steinbeck found in his Long Island garden, which contained three shirts, a bath towel, an arrow, and a rake.

The male plays hod carrier to the female's bricklayer. She has definite ideas about how things should be arranged and fulfills her task with zeal. The loose mass grows up and out until it looms like a giant mushroom cap against the horizon. Nest finished, the female turns broody, sitting deep in the nest cup so that only her head shows. The male brings her fish and often spells her while she perches nearby and consumes her meal head first, with a kind of horrible delicacy.

When I'm at a loss to explain some bit of bird biology or behavior I've observed, I turn to Arthur Cleveland Bent's mighty twenty-volume series on the *Life Histories of North American Birds*. (Bill Frech started acquiring copies of the books in the 1920s, when the U.S. Government Printing Office sent them out free. He got all but the last three volumes, which he had to buy from the publisher.) The organization of these volumes is tidy and pleasing. The section on ospreys, for instance, lists the bird's full Latin name, *Pandion haliaëtus carolinensis*. Then the common name, from the Latin *ossifraga*, or sea eagle. Then come sections filled with copious details on courtship, nesting, plumage, voice, enemies, and eggs, all enhanced by the observations of a large company of tipsters. Here's Mr. Clinton G. Abbott's catalogue of osprey calls:

> The commonest note is a shrill whistle, with a rising inflection: *Whew, whew, whew, whew, whew, whew, whew*. This is the sound usually heard during migration; and when the bird is only slightly aroused. When she becomes thoroughly alarmed it will be: *Chick, chick, chick, cheek, cheek, ch-cheek, ch-cheek, cheereek, chezeek, chezeek*, gradually increasing to a frenzy of excitement at the last. Another cry sounds like: *Tseep, tseep, tseep-whick, whick, whick-ick-ick-ck-ck*, dying away in a mere hiccough.

It is no easy task to record bird sound on paper, and you have to admire the efforts of Abbott. One crochety contributor expresses disappointment in this range: "All these notes . . . seem inadequate to express the emotions of so large a bird."

For the latest field studies on ospreys, I turn to Alan Poole's book, *Ospreys: A Natural and Unnatural History*. Here are hundreds of businesslike facts: the number of minutes of hunting necessary to meet the daily food requirements of an osprey family (195), the percentage of eggs lost from an average clutch in New York (68%) and in Corsica (21%), the total population of breeding pairs in Britain (45) and along the Chesapeake Bay (1,500).

According to both Bent and Poole, ospreys are traditional, one could even say conservative, birds. A female selects her mate not by his fancy flight, melodious song, or flamboyant feathers, but by his choice of homes. The birds favor the top limbs of large, mature, isolated trees. In a typical old-growth forest, fewer than one in a thousand trees suit. On this coast, where mature forests are mostly gone, the birds resort to distinctly unnatural sites: telephone poles, channel markers, fishing piers, and duck blinds. They favor overwater sites, which offer good protection from raccoons and other four-footed predators, but are of no use against winged carnivores such as the great horned owl. I've seen these formidable hunters perched on the Lewes water tower, heard them caterwauling in the dark, and found their pellets in the pine forest, packed solid with bones, feathers, and fur.

Ospreys are thought to mate for life. However, a recent story in *The New York Times* tells me that there is almost no such thing as true monogamy in the animal kingdom. It reports that scientists are uncovering evidence of philandering in species after species, withering the notion of lovingly coupled birds. With sophisticated spying techniques, they are spotting members of supposedly faithful pairs—purple martins, barn swallows, black-capped chickadees—flitting off for extramarital affairs. With DNA fingerprinting, they've compiled dossiers on the adulterers. One of the few known examples of true monogamy, they say, is a rodent living in the weeds and grasses of the midwestern prairies, a homely little vole called *Microtus ochrogaster*, which is utterly committed to its mate.

Still, it is fairly well established that adultery is rare among ospreys, and there are stories of fervent conjugal devotion. Bent reports the story of a bird whose mate was killed when a bolt of lightning struck her nest. The male refused to abandon the site, perching in a nearby tree all summer, a bird-shaped picture of bereavement. He returned the following year and stood vigil for another season.

A typical osprey clutch consists of three eggs, which Bent describes as "the handsomest of all the hawks' eggs . . . roughly the size of a hen's egg." Bent collected eggs most of his life, saved the orbs as trophies, laying their speckles in a cabinet fragrant with that peculiar pungent egg odor. "I shall never forget my envious enthusiasm," he writes, "when a rival boy collector showed me the first fish hawk's eggs I had ever seen." He goes on to describe the range of their appearance in loving detail: "The shell is fairly smooth and finely granulated. The ground color . . . may be white, creamy white, pinkish white, pale pinkish cinnamon, fawn color, light pinkish cinnamon, or vinaceous-cinnamon. They are usually heavily blotched and spotted with dark rich browns or bright reddish browns, bone brown, liver brown, bay, chestnut, burnt sienna, or various shades of brownish drab."

It was after reading this description that I bought a scope to watch more closely the activities of the ospreys nesting near King's Highway. I couldn't see the eggs themselves: They sat too low in the nest. But sometime late in the second week of June, they hatched. The newborn chicks were unfinished things, fuzzy flesh poking up from the bottom of the nest, as naked and helpless as a human baby, and no less perishably tender. Unlike such precocial birds as plovers and sandpipers, which go forth into the world straight from the egg, young ospreys take some coddling. Despite a steady stream of fish delivered by its parents, one chick died ten days later. The survivor, a fat squab with golden pinfeathers and thick black eye stripes, turned mobile at about four weeks, pestering its mother for fish and backing up now and again to squirt feces over the nest's edge. By midsummer, fatted on shad and flounder, puffed up on menhaden, it was flapping its scrawny wings, testing flight.

One warm, still day later that summer, I watched a young osprey fishing in the bay. The water was alive with hundreds of small silver fish that split the calm, sun-smooth surface. The bird flew in high from the southwest, slowly spiraled down to seventy or eighty feet, and began to stalk the shallows. The bright eye opened, the head lowered, the wings folded, then the feet thrust forward and the bird dropped like a feathered bomb, striking the water with a burst of spray.

Millions of generations of natural selection have made these birds good at what they do. Though ospreys have been known to take snakes, turtles, voles, and even baby alligators, 99 percent of their diet is fish, and they play every piscine angle. They spot fish from hundreds of feet above the water, even bottom fish with superb camouflage, like flounder. They penetrate the sun's glare or a dark, rippled water surface and adjust their strike to compensate for light refraction. With an eye membrane called a pecten, they change focus instantly to keep the fish in perfect view as they plunge. They hit the water at speeds of twenty to forty miles per hour. Their dense, compact plumage protects against the force of the impact; a flap of tissue on top of the beak closes over the nostrils to shut out the splash. The bird's strong, sinewy legs are superbly adapted for catching and holding slippery prey. Sharp talons, curved and of equal length, can snap shut in a fiftieth of a second. One toe swings back so that the osprey can clutch its prey with two claws on either side. Short spines on the base of the bird's toes and footpads ensure a firm grip.

With several deep wingbeats, this young bird rose slowly, shook its wings, and shifted the wildly flapping quiver of silver in its broad talons so that it rode headfirst, like a rudder. I watched until nothing could be seen of it but the dark V-sign of wings against the sky.

Aldo Leopold once wrote about the physics of beauty in the sand hills of Wisconsin. "Everybody knows . . . that the autumn landscape in the north woods is the land, plus a red maple, plus a ruffed grouse. In terms of conventional physics, the grouse represents only a millionth of either the mass or the energy of an acre. Yet subtract the grouse and the whole thing is dead. . . . A philosopher has called this imponderable essence the *numenon* of material things." For me, the osprey supplies the same kind of motive power to this place.

In the 1950s and '60s, this coast nearly lost its numenon to DDT, what Rachel Carson called the "elixir of death." March brought few homecomers, June grew no aerie. The toxic brew did more damage to the osprey than had been done by decades of egg collecting, hunting, and habitat destruction.

During World War II, the U.S. Army had used DDT to combat body lice among its troops, successfully breaking the chain of typhus infection. After the war, farmers and government workers began using the pesticide as a weapon against mosquitoes and agricultural pests. Its hazards were recognized from the beginning. Two researchers from the U.S. Fish and Wildlife Service published a paper in 1946 warning of the dangers of DDT. They had found that spraying in New Jersey endangered blue crabs. In Pennsylvania, it was brook trout; in

Maryland, birds, frogs, toads, snakes, and fish. Still, for almost three decades, most of the East Coast's shoreline and marshes were blanketed with DDT in an effort to eradicate the common salt-marsh mosquito. Long-lasting and easily dispersed, the pesticide spread over the earth in much the same pattern as radioactive fallout, carried aloft by wind and deposited on the ground in rainfall. By the 1960s, it permeated wildlife all around the globe, even lodging in tissues of Adélie penguins in Antarctica.

The highest concentrations of DDT residues were found in carnivorous birds at the top of the food chain: bald eagles, peregrine falcons, ospreys. The pesticide found its way into plankton and phytoplankton (microscopic plants and algae such as diatoms and dinoflagellates), which were eaten by shellfish, insects, and other creatures, which were eaten by fingerlings, which were in turn eaten by larger fish, which were caught by osprey. The concentration of the pesticide increased as much as ten times with each level in the chain. (Fish also accumulate toxins by absorbing pollutants directly through their gills.) What started out as a minute amount of DDT in water or plants ended up as a big dose in fish and an even bigger dose in the fatty tissues of birds of prey.

Ospreys can rid themselves of small amounts of some toxins: mercury, for instance. They excrete it from the blood into growing feathers, which are eventually molted—a technique that works only during the molting season. But mercury occurs in nature; DDT is man-made. Birds have had no time to evolve a way to rid their bodies of the poison. As the toxin accumulates in fatty tissues, it blocks the efficient metabolism of calcium and so makes the shell of an osprey's egg brittle, cracked by a touch of fingers. When a female settles down to incubate, she crushes her clutch beneath her.

Around the turn of the century, the ornithologist Alexander Wilson remarked that he saw osprey "thick about Rehoboth Bay," some twenty nests within a half-mile range. A concentrated colony flourished then at Cape Henlopen, with twenty-three nesting pairs, probably drawn by the dense schools of menhaden that crowded the waters of the lower bay. By 1972, when DDT was finally banned in the United States, populations of ospreys here and elsewhere along the northeast coast had plummeted to a small fraction of their former numbers. When Bill Frech came to Lewes in 1977, there were forty-six nesting pairs of osprey in all of Delaware. That year, observers across the bay at Cape May counted just over a thousand migrating osprey during the whole autumn season. Since the 1970s, the birds have somehow recovered their numbers. In October of 1989, nearly a thousand birds were spotted passing through Cape May on a single day. At last count, Delaware had seventy-five nests.

Most ospreys along this coast make impressive annual migrations in orbit with the seasons, traveling south to the tropics in fall and north again in spring to breed. Young birds travel both ways alone. The migration route they follow is not learned, but acquired in the egg, carried in them by the accident of ancestry. A young osprey fledged in Lewes goes south to Peru or Venezuela to winter in the hot mists and vast swamps of the Amazon, and returns after a year or two to breed on the very same stretch of temperate shore where it fledged.

I know the gift of being able to find home is not allotted merely to these birds. Moose return annually to the same summer range. Bears transported more than fifty miles from their territory come back to it within days. Something in the cold

Osprey eggs in nest

brains of sea turtles guides them to their natal beaches after prodigious migrations of thousands of miles. Even limpets seem to know their way home, crawling back to a favorite scar or dimple on a rock at low tide, even if the face of the rock they cross has been hammered or chiseled into oblivion. Terns, swallows, gulls, and song sparrows, as well as shore-birds—piping plovers, ruddy turnstones, and sanderlings—all return to the same nesting ground in what is called *ortstreue*, or "place faithfulness." A strong attachment to birthplace makes good biological sense, of course. In a familiar landscape, animals have an easier time finding nesting sites and prey and avoiding predators. Biologist Ernst Mayr once remarked that birds have wings not so much for the purpose of getting away to a place but for the purpose of getting home.

Still, it seems astonishing that a young osprey, only a few months old, can take off over land and water and travel south three thousand miles; then, years later, head sure and direct, without guidance, back to the precise point of its infancy. Scientists believe that members of a pair stay together because they share a deep affinity for the same stretch of marsh or shore. Apparently ospreys carry an image of home in their heads that is sharp and well defined. How does a young bird register this place? What are its landmarks of sight and smell? Is it, as Lamarck said, that the environment creates the organ? Does our particular wash of blue and white bore those bright golden eyes and code the neurons that stream into those kinked wings? Do our mottled currents and patterns of marsh grass brand a bird, saying, Come toward this shore? There may be other sensual messages sent by the earth, undetected by us, but which a bird is innately prepared to receive. Although scientists suspect that some consciousness of the exact magnetic topology and field strength of a nesting area has something to do with it, no one really knows. "It's a black box sort of thing," one ornithologist told me. Somehow this stretch of shore works a kind of magic against all others to pull its progeny from the sky.

When I was twelve, the school I went to sat on a hillside near a mature deciduous wood. At lunchtime, I often retreated to a small clearing some distance from the school to eat my sandwich and reflect on the morning's events. One day I sat on a log, peeling bark from a stick, and pondering the news that had struck our family a few weeks before: my father was leaving my mother. It was a warm, breezy day. Sunlight moving in and out of the clouds shattered the leafy surfaces with flecks of gold. I hadn't noticed trouble between my parents, engrossed as I was in my own awkward passing into adolescence. No shouting, no slamming doors. Suddenly this. The sunglasses my mother had been wearing for days couldn't conceal from me her wet face, her bafflement and sense of betrayal. I was at that age when I yearned above all else to be invisible, the way a Fowler's toad is invisible against the sand of the pine forest floor. The rift between my parents made me stand out and pick sides. It set me adrift, hunting for stable sanctuary in what had come to seem a shifting, unreliable world.

These woods were comforting and familiar. I knew their mossy hummocks and decaying stumps as well as any place I'd ever known. But this day I saw something new. Glancing up from the stick in my hand, I noticed a vibrating white dot about the size of a firefly in the trunk of an oak tree some distance from where I sat. It was more an absence than a presence, a tiny pulsating hole. I stared and stared. The hole slowly grew into a crescent, then a large ragged horseshoe, a sizeable bite that should have split the tree in two. But the top half of the trunk just hung there like a stalactite. Still the hole grew, spreading in pulses until it swallowed nearby bushes and trees in white-hot light. It was as if my woods were being punched out or sucked up in a shiny boiling void. I couldn't shift my gaze from the growing hole, and a sense of horror stole over me. I got up and stumbled blindly out of the woods. By this time my hands were numb, dead weight at the ends of my arms, like dangling lumps of dough. Nausea roiled my insides, then a dot of hot pain shot through my temple and set the right side of my head throbbing.

This was my first experience with the aura of a classical migraine headache. The visual disturbance, the scintillating, zigzaggy chasm, is called a scotoma, meaning darkness or shadow. I rarely have such attacks anymore. I've learned to fend them off by lying down in darkness and focusing on that first tiny flash of white light, concentrating it until it shrinks into a pinpoint and pops out of existence. But I still think of that first aura not merely as a chaotic burst of firing among the thin wires of my brain but as a sudden, complete extinction of place.

Oddly enough, that pleat in my perception held a vision of the future. Several years later, when I returned to visit those woods, I found them gone. In their place was a thick cluster of row houses that clung like barnacles to the edge of the hill, and I was struck anew by a sense of disorientation and loss.

This sensation is not peculiar to humans. The loss of familiar surroundings, the destruction of refuge, is no doubt felt by animals, perhaps even more keenly than by our kind. I once saw something like this happen to a pair of osprey that for more than a decade had nested on a dilapidated pier behind the old fish factories. The pier was used in the 1950s and '60s to offload the giant nets of menhaden. When the factories closed, the pier fell into disuse; all that was left was a set of rotting pilings with a few cross timbers, disconnected from the land. One fall, developers bulldozed the fish factories to build condominiums and tore up the old pier. When the osprey returned that March, I watched them circle the empty water for hours in bewilderment. They hung around for days, perching on a nearby utility pole and watching the site, apparently recollecting a structure now made of air.

Stories are told of species that retain an image in their heads of places that have long disappeared. Monarchs migrating over Lake Superior fly south, then east, then south again, as if reading the echoes of a long-vanished glacier. Year after year, pilot whales on their autumn migrations strand themselves on the beaches of Cape Cod, as if unwilling to accept the presence of a twelve-thousand-year-old geological upstart that has parked itself in the middle of a migratory path they have followed for millions of years. American toads return to breed in ponds that have long since been paved over, drawn by some insubstantial vapor, some aura of home.

Studies of human preferences for landscapes have found that our tribe tends to favor savannalike land—flat, grass-covered landscape studded with trees, where we had our origins and earliest home. Also promontories overlooking water. Some scientists even speculate that somewhere along the way we veered off the common primate course of evolution not just by swinging down from trees, but by going toward the sea. The seashore, with its abundance of edibles—fish, mollusks, turtle and bird eggs, digestible plants—and of shells, vines, kelp, and driftwood for tools, was the home of emergent humanity.

I like this idea that our earliest home landscapes are buried deep, embedded in our minds like an anchor at great depth, that we know in some dark, birdly way where we want to go.

Beauty may, indeed, lie in the genes of the beholder. Ospreys have been around for something like fifteen million years, long before we ever set foot on seashores. In our burgeoning minds, shore has never been separate from bird, so perhaps at some level, the two are joined in an inexplicable sweetness of union. Perhaps the osprey exists on a mental map of an earlier world passed down from our ancestors, and the bird in its landscape enters us like the parental. Perhaps it is also the other way around: Perhaps *he* contains *us* as part of his element, having seen us through the ages, through our infancy and the whole tumult of civilized man.

I wonder, too, if the residues of old ancestral landscapes

don't rise up in our minds by the same deep grooves that make the scent of hay or sunlit ferns call up an episode from child-hood, so that we act on buried instinct—like a dog at the hearth who turns slowly around and around on himself, tamp-ing down a circle of imaginary grass—so that for the sake of marking her union in a meaningful way, a young bride puts up with salt stench and sand in her shoe.

Who placed us with eyes between a
microscopic and a telescopic world?
—*Henry David Thoreau*

Between

Tides

$\mathcal{J}$f one were compiling a list of Unpromising Landscapes, the mud flats of the cape might be one. At low tide the brown gullied plain looks barren, its only features being wave-carved ridges and a skin of algal scum. Strewn about are the wrecks of shelled creatures: false angel wings, scallops, mussels, razor clams, hardshell clams, dwarf tellins, ocellated lady crabs, rock crabs. Hollow barnacles encrust the bulbous shell of a spider crab with no trace of legs. A smack of jellyfish have stranded on the sand, mostly comb jellies and saucer-shaped moon jellies, their pink gonads arranged like a flower at the heart of the clear quivering mass. I'm reminded of my first encounter with a tide flat, when I was taken as a child to dig for clams at the Maryland shore. Everything about the experience made my flesh creep: the dark ooze, the dead jellies, the smell of salt twined with the tang of rot. A large limp crab rose and fell in the surf. It had a single claw like a mouth and a sharp, speckled red shell from which projected black pinpoint eyes that ogled the shore. Swarms of flies came up and out of nowhere to sting my legs and face. The place seemed sinister and lifeless, like an open grave.

This morning, on swash bars toward the tip of the cape, a company of herring gulls are roosting in a loose flock. One stands apart near the water's edge. It cocks its head from side to side and lifts its feet, first one, then the other, paddling the soft sand in a rhythmic one-two beat. Turtles do this, too, stomping the ground with their heavy pads. The vibrations bring earthworms to the surface. This gull is stirring up something, making it visible by making it move. It's out to catch a meal. I'm out to glimpse the hive of life beneath this crust of shells and grassy scum.

Tidal flats such as these harbor as many as three hundred species: shrimps, crabs, clams, worms, all dual citizens in a country sometimes land, sometimes sea. The worms, especially, interest me. Soft-bodied and bare of any shell or case, they have traded the freedom of life in the open for the dark safety of a tube or burrow. In a sunless, labyrinthine city live bloodworms, mud worms, lugworms, tube worms, bamboo worms, acorn worms, and plumed worms—strikingly colored with iridescent skin and scarlet gills—all variations on a good, functional vermiform theme that took nature a billion years to develop.

If I kneel to scrutinize the surface closely, tiny clear tubes about a millimeter in diameter emerge from the dry rise of the sand bars. These belong to the glassy tube worm, a small, slender creature I've yet to see, with a pair of long, curling palps on its head. Nearby, little black chimneys poke up about an inch or two. Roughly the size of a thin cigar and hooked like a shepherd's crook, they are shaggy with bits of shells, tiny

Plumed worms and glassy tube worms

stones, seaweed, and sticks collected by the plumed worm to festoon the public part of its home and to attract the small animals that constitute its dinner. (The private part of the tube is bare and reaches below the surface as much as three feet.) In the tide pools are the thin fecal rods and pellets of the red-gilled mud worm, and an occasional coil like a flattened brioche, the signature of the acorn worm. I saw one of these once in a laboratory, a lovely, luckless creature drowned in a petri dish—tricolored, with a pale pink proboscis, burnt orange collar, and body like a brown wrinkled suit.

"In searching for worms," says zoologist Augusta Foote, "the digger must be quick and expert." A shallow drive with my shovel yields only a soupy hole that fills as fast as I can empty it. A deeper thrust turns up a solid lump of sediment, embroidered with a whitish worm. So! But just as I raise my shovel, the tip of the worm suddenly detaches and wriggles away like a minnow. Milky ribbon worms let go their tail part when disturbed, presumably to distract predators while the head end of the worm digs back into the sand. (The pink ribbon worm, a relative, splits into half a dozen sausagelike pieces, each of which becomes a whole, even if the fragment is only a tiny fraction of the original beast. It is as if the evolution of these worms took the shovel into account.)

I had read about the milky ribbon worm. Soft, smooth, slimy, several feet long, it is a nemertean, "the unerring one." It eats other worms, small crustaceans, and mollusks. At night it swims the waters of high tide, undulating like an eel. By day it gropes through the dark sand, producing peristaltic waves along its body to launch underground attacks on its prey. One day while wandering the flats, I noticed a razor clam sticking up from the sand. Though these clams feed near the surface at high tide, they usually withdraw into their burrows as the waters ebb, and they have a way of descending even deeper at approaching footsteps, digging down rapidly with a powerful cylindrical foot. This one didn't budge. I stepped closer. At last I crouched down on the wet sand and reached over to touch the clam's glossy brown shell. It moved its tiny siphons. Still it did not retreat. I suspect it was gripped by a vermicular assassin.

The milky ribbon worm is no tender carnivore. It approaches from below. From a pore at the front of its head, it shoots out a tubular, threadlike proboscis, as long or longer than its body, and entraps its prey in coils sticky with a thick, toxic mucus. Opening a slitlike mouth, elastic enough to engulf large animals, it slides up the clam like a stocking, then rapidly digests the sweet protruding flesh. The clam, for its part, is stuck between jetting upward out of its burrow toward the sharp death of shorebirds, or moving downward deeper into the gut of the worm.

Another thrust of the shovel unearths a perfect little cone-shaped tube about three inches long. At the wide end is a comb of golden bristles, which caps the mottled blue and red body of the trumpet worm. A master mason, this worm constructs an architectural wonder out of a single layer of sand grains. Using a pair of tentacles, it selects and sorts the grains, then precisely fits them so that the smaller ones lie at the narrow end of the cone and the heftier ones at the wide end. The worm lies head down and feeds on microbe-coated sand from the bottom of the tube. Only the tip of the cone protrudes above the surface for breathing.

The trumpet worm lives alone in the dark neighborhood beneath this plain, but most residents have formed strange associations. The lugworm shares its U-shaped lodging with a round pea crab only a half-inch long. The bamboo worm, a brick-red, ribbed species, draws an ark of other animals to its long, sand-encrusted tube: mud snails, turret snails, parasitic snails, tiny symbiotic crustaceans, and a shiny white clam less than a fifth of an inch in length. As the worm feeds from the bottom of its tube, it creates a small hollow, a microhabitat complete with a ventilating water current. Here the little clam lodges, enjoying a life nearly free from predation and an abundant source of food, which it strains from the tube water.

Some of these couplings stretch the definition of neighborly relations. One small, delicate shore shrimp, so transparent you can see eggs through its body, harbors a crustacean, a kind of isopod that settles in the shrimp's gill and forms a large blister-like bulge there.

In ancient Greek, the word "parasite" meant "one who eats at the table of another." One trematode parasite living on these flats has lost its table manners. It resides for a time in the flesh of mud snails, feeding voraciously all the while on its host's nutritious flesh, gobbling up glands and gonads. The trematodes also release a chemical that shapes the behavior of the beleaguered snail, prodding it to leave the low wet swales of its customary habitat and crawl up to dry beaches at nighttime high tide. The larvae of the trematodes then emerge from the bodies of the snails to infect the beach fleas that frequent the region at night. Shorebirds descend in the morning to eat the fleas, parasites and all. Once the larvae enter a bird's guts, they mature and produce eggs that are released onto the flats with the bird's feces, and the cycle begins anew.

An organ like a pink tongue thrusts forward from the sediment, lingers briefly, then retreats. I dare not excavate further if I want to see the whole beast. The acorn worm is so flaccid that it fragments at the least disturbance. Its business is this: mining helical burrows and eating sand. I've watched the worms at work in a kind of artificial farm of sand and saltwater built in a laboratory at the University of Delaware. The worm's proboscis, covered with a sticky slime, pokes from one end of the burrow and probes the surface of the sand, collecting grains, which it passes to a mouth just beneath its collar. The organ retreats, then extends again. With probe after probe, it traces a perfect rosette surrounding the hole. Each day an acorn worm eats up to three hundred times its body weight in sand. Only a tiny fraction of what it takes in is food—microbes and other organic matter. Every so often it backs up and defecates the rest in little mounds on the surface. After the sand pellet is expelled, it is rapidly recolonized by microbes and before long is again suitable for consumption. Along creeks and bays from Maine to North Carolina, acorn worms are tilling the sand the way earthworms work a garden. The cape's flats have a population of roughly four million worms. That comes to an average daily turnover of three tons of sediment, all leavened and renewed.

Edward O. Wilson has said that every species is like a magic well: The more you draw from it, the more there is to draw. So it is with the acorn worm. Its heart lies in its proboscis; its faint consciousness is stretched throughout its body. Scientists have found that it uses a good share of its energy and resources to make massive amounts of a toxic chemical similar in structure and composition to Agent Orange and DDT. The substance may repel fish and predators. These sands are laced with thousands of pounds of it.

No doubt there are chemical messages dashed all over the flats. So much slips through the coarse net of my senses. When I crunch one of the mud snails that cobble the furrows of this plain, it releases a chemical alarm, a whiff of fear that makes neighboring snails within a couple of feet burrow deep or flee. To the snail, freshly killed crabs or fish are scent beacons broadcasting signals of food. Mud snails quickly detect the amino acids that leach from these creatures. The lobsters that wander this shore in winter go the snail one better. Their bodies are covered with odor-sensitive receptors that detect minute concentrations of pheromones, chemicals they use for nearly every activity from tracking prey to announcing sexual prowess. Thin hairs on their attennules have more than four hundred different kinds of receptor cells, each tuned to a specific chemical compound. Just as birds can distinguish myriad notes packed into a brief musical interval, lobsters can read a spectrum of chemicals in a teaspoon of seawater.

* * *

Warm fingers of foamy water are slowly creeping inland, tiny translations of the giant movement of the tides. As the sea travels over the ribbed bottom of the flats, fish move in from the deep, dissolving in and out of sight around my feet. Though they seem mute, they are not. They fill the waters with belches and cries, calls of courtship, alarm, aggression, and fright. A researcher named Dr. Marie Poland Fish once auditioned every species of North Atlantic coastal fish she could collect and found that they thump, cluck, croak, bark, rasp, hiss, growl, swish, spit, scratch, and quack. Eels bubble and thud. Herrings signal in soft chirps. Sea robins squawk, toadfish grunt, and striped bass utter an "unk." During World War II, croakers in the Chesapeake Bay made such an underwater rumpus with their rhythmic chugging that they fooled the coastal defense network into thinking it was under invasion.

Some fish produce their sounds by grinding teeth or rasping spines, but most are percussionists. They make a drumming noise by contracting special muscles on each side of a resonating air bladder. Nearly all fish experience a deepening of their voice as they grow, except the trout, which remains a treble all of its life. Sound travels well underwater, almost five times faster than it moves through air, but the vibrations have an amplitude too narrow for our ears. (I was intrigued to read that the pitch at which human ears are most sensitive is that of a child's cry.) Fish, with their inner ear and lines of tiny motion-sensitive hairlike sensors running along both sides of their bodies, blend hearing and touch, sensing liquid sounds well beyond my range.

As I wade through the rising flood, a shadow of minnows flicks in and out, scaring before my stride. All around me life begins to feed beneath the water's glinting lid. The razor clam thrusts up its siphon to suck a stream of water. The tiny crab spreads its feathery attennae to filter minute life that wafts past it. The plumed worm pumps food through its tube, and the ribbon worm swims off to search for its third meal of the day. Crabs hunt clams, fish hunt shrimp, worms hunt clams and other worms in a landscape as noisy, as active as any. But I hear no clash or snarl.

We humans are an eye-minded lot, and even this sense is bested by some tide flat organisms. Along the southeastern edge of this continent lives a large but elusive crustacean, a fierce predator known as the mantis shrimp. Pale green, up to a foot long and robust of build, it is a sort of souped-up version of its insect namesake, with a large pair of powerful claws that it folds beneath its body. These claws snap out to strike rivals or seize prey in one of the fastest animal movements ever recorded: six milliseconds from start to bloody finish. The shrimp's prey is worms, snails, clams, crabs, and fishes, which it easily detects with a pair of large, stalked emerald eyes. The eye cells in some mantis shrimps have ten color-sensitive pigments. The cones in our eyes have only three, with which we can distinguish five million gradations of color. To my eyes, a scallop's shell is watery pink, its mantle rimmed with eyes of blue. What does a mantis shrimp see? A shell with myriad shades of salmon, peach, rose, ochre, all distinct and distinguishable hues? Eyes a gamut of azure, indigo, cobalt where I see just blue?

The first step of Copernicus, wrote Jacob Bronowski, was "to lift himself from the earth and put himself wildly, speculatively into the sun." There he could see that the earth conceives from the sun, and the sun rules the family of planets. To study genes that jump from one chromosome to another, the great geneticist Barbara McClintock descended into her subject. The more she worked with the chromosomes, "the bigger [they] got," she said, "and when I was really working with them I wasn't outside, I was down there. I was part of the system. . . . I actually felt as if . . . these were my friends." It's what she calls having "a feeling for the organism."

Some naturalists find this vision at an early age. Their ability to focus deeply on other organisms emerges of its own accord or is nudged to the fore by the prompting of a mentor. The minds of young Darwin, Audubon, Nuttall, and entomologist Jean-Henri Fabre were filled to the limits with intense consciousness of worms, birds, plants, and ants. "As far back as I can remember," wrote Fabre, "I see myself in ecstasy before the splendour of a Ground-beetle's wingcases or the wings of *Papilio machaon*, the Swallowtail." Miriam Rothschild, an expert on fleas, once wrote of her childhood summers on a farm in Hungary. She could not remember the family-filled house or the neighbors, only the nest of a long-tailed tit, a ditch lined with violets, the moths that gathered at her nightlight. "I was greatly puzzled by the strange way the lappet moth hunkered down," she wrote. "Where was its head?"

Among the earliest memories of ornithologist George M. Sutton were these: a collection of bird skins he saw when he was three—"row upon row, drawer after drawer, of red-winged blackbirds, jays, orioles, tanagers, hawks, owls, sandpipers"—and an incident with his father. The two were standing on an iron bridge over the swollen waters of the Mississippi River. A blackbird lighted on the railing. Sutton's father lifted the boy up to stand on the railing and suggested that the bird, perched in this pose, felt no fear.

To sway outside yourself and dwell in other lives. I think of this ability as a sort of specialized muscle, kept firm only by use. It grows soft from neglect. But the nerve that fires it never flags, even in those of us who are not born naturalists, who had no childhood passion for ants, no uncle with a drawer full of butterflies. That nerve is an ancient, instinctive kinship for wild things, which fires right on down a life. It may be the quickening that comes with seeing a flight of snow geese pink-bellied in the western sun or a mouse so close you can sense the warm rapid tick of its tiny pulse.

Humans, says astronomer Harlow Shapley, lie midway between the sun and the atom, both in grams of mass and in centimeters of diameter. Narrow is the world with whose dimensions our lives, our limbs, our senses are in tune. So much that matters is invisible by the yardstick of human life. How to shatter scale-bound thinking, see more deeply, widely? Writers such as Lewis Carroll have defamiliarized the world in this way, made us see our surroundings in strange new light. Think of swimming in a sea of tears, rolling with a worm in a giant peach. Think of Blake, a world in a grain of sand, eternity in an hour. There is a deep hunch here, more than meets the eye.

I scoop up a handful of wet sand from my feet, a lump that has likely passed through the guts of innumerable worms. The grains have distant origins and rich history. Derived from the weathering of ancient continental granite over thousands of years, they are colorless quartz and pink feldspar, mixed with a light crush of shells and tiny fragments of heavy minerals, zircon, amphibole, and garnet, which suggest the sand's source—igneous and metamorphic rocks from the Piedmont Province to the west. The great bulk is quartz, among the hardest of minerals at Earth's surface. After years of grinding by waves, quartz breaks down to round, polished crystals that are nearly indestructible.

Spread a few grains under a microscope, and an exotic world is revealed, close, breezeless, color-charged in spots, like the pink moon of Neptune. A film of moisture surrounds and separates the grains. In these tiny watery capillaries is a riot of life: insects, copepods, ostracods, nematodes, protozoa, gastrotrichs, and tardigrades—called water bears on account of their little claws and short, stumpy legs—each organism measured in microns and exquisitely suited to the microhabitat in which it swims, feeds, and multiplies. These are the meiofauna (from the Greek meaning "smaller"), a diverse group of creatures with a representative from nearly every phylum in the animal kingdom. In a sense they put the rest of shore life in the shade. On almost any intertidal flat, you can expect to find millions of these organisms per square meter of sediment surface.

If I put my handful of sand in a bucket, cover it with seawater, knead it for a few minutes, then pour the wash water into a small jar, with a lens I can see some of these animalcules, writhing, gliding, lashing from side to side, jitterbugging to the bottom of the jar. But most are well beyond the resolution of my glass. They tend to be less than a millimeter long, camouflaged and slender, the better to slip through narrow waterways without dislodging the sand grains. They are more simplified than their larger relatives, with one testis instead of two, or a stomach made of only a few cells in place of the usual thousand.

The most abundant are the nematodes, long worms tapered at both ends. They live everywhere from nearly dry dune sand to beach with heavy surf, and often make up at least half the total number of meiofauna in any given place. Some have a joint mid-body, like an ant's waist, and move like inchworms, alternately attaching front and hind end to a sand grain. Inching represents a fine solution to a problem in physics. Their world is ruled not by the forces of gravity, but by electromagnetic attractions between molecules. For a nematode, a grain of sand is a boulder and the moist film around it, a viscous sea about the consistency of honey. In a world that frequently turns topsy-turvy, meiofauna have evolved sundry bizarre ways of coping. Lacking visual cues, many have specialized receptors to tell them which way is down. To get where it's going, one kind of gastrotrich has a pair of sticky, handlike organs near its head, and a branched toe in the rear. Ostracods make an adhesive thread to secure themselves to a sand grain and scale it like a mountain climber. Parenting is tricky. Most of these organisms produce few eggs, usually clutches of ten or less. Some make eggs that are sticky enough to adhere to sand grains. Others incubate their eggs in a brood pouch, not releasing the young until they're fully independent. In one wormlike species, embryos remain attached to the mother's rear end and develop while she tows them about.

The smallest meiofauna are the rotifers. Descended from a larger ancestor in a rare reversal of the usual evolutionary trend, they are the smallest multicelled animals, with a pear-shaped body, head topped by a wreath of cilia (which they use to feed and move), and two small, pointed, sticky toes bringing up the rear. Utterly translucent, they are little essays in obscurity: How to Be Unseen.

Many of these beings have an ability to hunker down when conditions get too cold, dry, or otherwise rough. Under a microscope, dry sand looks completely barren, but saturate that sand with water and you'll witness a silent explosion. Nematodes hatch from eggs. Protozoa spring awake from a dormant state. Tardigrades swell out of deathlike granules to resume life.

Hold in mind this turmoil of energies, all these births and deaths and expert adaptations, the minute munching and silent sucking multiplied a million, trillionfold, and this mud flat begins to take new shape.

There is more. Still smaller are the minute single-celled organisms, among them bacteria and diatoms, poised in the watery capillaries or stuck to the surface of sand grains. A single grain of sand can support hundreds of colonies of bacteria, each composed of hundreds of individuals, as well as twenty or thirty diatoms of different varieties—all residing in the craters, scarps, and troughs of the grain, where they are protected from abrasion as the sand knocks about. Up to five million bacteria might live in a single milliliter of sand. Though small in size and extremely short-lived (with life lasting a matter of minutes), theirs is a big wedge of the intertidal pie. By making nutrients out of dead organic matter, bacteria supply food for meiofauna, amphipods, shrimps, worms, and myriad other organisms. So do diatoms. Like most plants, these have photosynthetic pigments that make food with light. Sunshine pours into the single cell of the diatom, then passes into the gastrotrich, the razor clam, the milky ribbon worm.

Diatoms are plants unlike any I've seen before, so small they have no common names. Their single cell is enclosed within a two-part shell of silica. Under the microscope, these shells are beautiful, intricately sculptured with pits, pores, spines, ribs, and spindles. The ones most common in these waters are like tiny glass houses linked together in a train.

Though invisible to the naked eye, diatoms are as alive as

Diatoms found at the mouth of the Delaware Bay

the fig tree in my neighbor's yard and perhaps more sensitive to their surroundings. Normal communities have a large number of different species, each with special needs of oxygen, light, and temperature. When conditions change in a place, so do the diatoms that live there. In this way, they serve as tiny environmental barometers. Drill a core in the earth, study the fossil diatoms, and you'll find a telling record.

At Rehoboth Bay, a few miles south of here, a geologist drilled down a couple of feet to sediment that lay on the surface three centuries ago. What she found was this: The deepest, oldest sample contained more than seventy kinds of diatoms, among them, large numbers of *Cymatosira belgica*, a species found on clean, sandy beaches. In the next sample up, marking a lapse of a hundred years, a time when new human settlements in the region were thriving, the number of species had dropped to sixty. *C. belgica* had lost its hold to a variety that likes turbidity and needs little light.

Higher up in the core was a layer marking a period around 1870, soon after the first chemical fertilizer plant was built in Baltimore. Farmers all over the Northeast had pioneered the use of artificial fertilizers and cleared more of their land for farming. The diversity of species declined again, and the numbers of those species that love nutrients and dim light suddenly exploded. Fifty years later came a boom in human population and with it large discharges of sewage. At the corresponding layer in the core, the number of diatom species dropped to the lowest ever: forty-four. The youngest wedge, from the top skin of soil, again harbored nearly sixty species, but of different varieties from those farther down in the sample, suggesting that something more than fertilizers, sewage, and soil runoff was affecting the plant communities. The geologist suspects toxins.

Though most diatoms live in water, they also grow on sand, rocks, plants, and animals, including the body feathers of diving seabirds and the skin of whales. Some diatoms expand like miniature forests on the surfaces they colonize, with long-stalked varieties forming canopies, while others create shrubs and field layers. Sand grain species have short stalks and resemble lemons. Few stay put. Those that live in mud flats tend to migrate up and down in synchrony with the tides. At daytime low tide, each tiny organism exudes mucus through pores at one end of its glassy cell wall, which jet-propels it upward to the surface, where it remains throughout ebb tide to bathe its photosynthetic cell in sunlight. With the rising tide, it descends to avoid grazing animals. The rhythms are not caused by the tides themselves; they originate from within. A scientist who experimented with diatoms found that even when they are lifted from the shore and kept in a laboratory under con-

stant conditions of light and temperature, their migratory patterns continue uninterrupted, occurring fifty minutes later each
day, faithful to the tides. Peer through one end of the scope or
the other: This plain seems boundless toward the great and
boundless toward the small.

The

Crab's

Tail

$\mathcal{I}$f I walk through town in the small hours of the morning, I can see lights or the flicker of television sets in the back bedrooms of my elderly neighbors. Lewes is filled with the ranks of those who have come to the sea to finish out their lives. There is the milder climate, of course, the tempered seasons and washed sea air. In the sea-molded curves and wide open space is release from harsh lines and corners, medicine for cramped places. In blue water and white sand there is the sense of things stripped clean, the big tabula rasa. There is comfort in the ticking meter of the sea, perhaps, and in returning to an environment for which we were all originally suited and which still lies slumbering somewhere deep inside us. Perhaps, too, there is release from reminders of youth. Conrad said that no man ever saw the sea looking young. "But some of us, regarding the ocean with understanding and affection, have seen it looking old, as if the immemorial ages had been stirred up from the undisturbed bottom of ooze."

I awake before dawn one morning and dress in the dark. The sand is cold on the short path to the beach. I turn left along the surf and head toward the bay side of the cape. A spring storm the night before has left the air fresh and the sea still fretful with long black rollers. In the dim light a few objects catch my eye, several pimpled pink starfish and the white gleam of a fish belly-up, that tender white of things that rarely or never see light.

Rounding the cape, I can just make out the figure of a man moving along the wrack line, bending and rising, bending and rising. We close on each other and he nods to me. "Thought I'd be alone at this hour." He might be seventy-five or eighty. He wears baggy trousers, a loose cardigan, and a wool knit cap over a mop of iron gray hair, and he carries a large burlap bag, wet through at the bottom. He has come out early, he says, to collect before the crowds arrive. He takes only driftwood and abandoned shells, not like the professional hunters who dig out live whelks or conchs and cut the glistening inhabitant from its home like a tongue from a mouth. He shows me a few of his shells, which are beautiful. Then he continues on his way, moving with speed and precision, with bewitching ease, like an athlete. I wonder how long he has been working in the dark.

A bright yellow band appears on the horizon. The light quickens. Beached on the sand is a tiny squid, soft and flaccid. A large wave strikes the shore, shoots up to the squid and then reverses, dragging the limp carcass toward the sea. I bend down over the wrack with a vague childish pleasure, batting away at the web of gnats, my face sticky with salt and airborne algae. Here's a signpost reduced to driftwood:

FISCH
ENTERPRI
NITROGEN

which must have migrated here from the old fish factories around the cape, and on it, a lovely white beetle with brown stripes—but I'm so entomologically ignorant that I can't identify what is probably a common species. Amid the nets of seaweed are whelk egg cases, chips on a string filled with hundreds of infant whelks no bigger than bird seed, and tiny cuticles of broken shells so thin they're translucent. I love the transformations wrought by the sea, the driftwood bleached to weightless white, shards of glass ground soft and hazy. As if beauty might come of anything. From time to time I catch a glimpse of a magnificent shell rolling in the breakers and leap into the surf to salvage it. A good shell can distill time and place, like a good poem, and seems worth wet feet. However, the thrill of discovery always carries with it a tinge of guilt at disturbing some evolving still-life at the edge. Pluck a shell from its matrix of gnats and seaweed, import it to a mantelpiece, and its power ebbs.

I once saw a set of seashell X rays, skeletal images of a chambered nautilus, a wentletrap, a sundial, and a slit shell. Though each shell has a radically different exterior, a common growth pattern emerged in the ghostly images of their carbonate forms. Mollusks make shells by extracting calcium from seawater to form calcium cabonate crystals, which they deposit at the mouth of the shell opening through laborious secretions. Some of their ancient ancestors built tubelike shells, long, straight, and cumbersome. Over the course of time, many mollusks evolved cones that coiled round a vertical axis in an elegant solution to the problem of too much armor. So in the sundial as in the slit shell, the spiral prevails. In X-ray image, the successive coils of the wentletrap do not touch one another, but are joined by thin delicate traceries of sculptural ribs. So highly prized was this shell in eighteenth-century

Europe that forgers created fine handcrafted imitations from rice paste.

Moving along the wrack line, I'm drawn by the air of mystery that surrounds the objects. The seastar, the whale skull, the clouded glass: Each has its own individual history, nearly always unknown, often unimaginable. This worm-eaten timber, for instance, might have been afloat for years, a tossed-up loss from some dead ship buried under miles of gray water. It's not so unlikely. This beach is haunted by ships grounded on the nearby shoals and smashed to pieces in rough weather.

"Every sinking generates its own aura," says writer James Hamilton-Patterson. The sinking of the H.M.S. *DeBraak* is no exception, having stirred the imaginations of people in Lewes for generations. It was a brief squall like the one last night that struck the *DeBraak* two hundred years ago and sank her a mile northwest of Cape Henlopen. A two-masted brig in the employ of the Royal Navy, one of those warships nicknamed "the wooden walls of England," she was rumored to be carrying eighty thousand pounds of gold coins, bars, precious stones, and other booty plundered from Spanish ships. She was heading for anchorage at the mouth of the bay when the storm struck, and a sudden flaw of wind laid her down. Water poured through open hatches, and she went straight to the bottom, taking with her Captain James Drew, thirty-four crew members, and several Spanish prisoners.

Drew's body floated ashore three days later and was buried in the cemetery of St. Peter's Church on the corner of Market and Second streets, just down the block from my house. Near his grave is the tomb of Captain Henry F. McCracken, a river pilot who was buried in 1868 along with his anchor. (Part of the iron fluke still protrudes from the ground.) It was Henry who thought to write down in the family Bible a compass bearing on the wreck of the *DeBraak*, which his father, Gilbert, had taken from the Cape Henlopen lighthouse at ebb tide, when—some say—the ship's masts were still above water.

Over the next two centuries, at least a dozen attempts were made to find the *DeBraak* using McCracken's bearing, but the ship had two defenses: a confusion over her exact location stemming from McCracken's failure to take a second bearing on the site, and murky waters with a five-knot tidal current that made diving difficult. In the spring of 1984 a professional diver from Rhode Island named Harvey Harrington finally found the wreck in eighty feet of water with the help of side-scan sonar, a system that emits sound pulses in two slanting fan-shaped beams, which are reflected by irregularities on the sea bottom. Over the next two years, Harrington's efforts to salvage the ship and its treasure took on the characteristics of a mad quest and drove the man deep into debt. Ahab had his whale, Harrington his *DeBraak*. From the depths, divers brought up artifact after artifact—a man's wig made of human hair, complete with an eighteenth-century queue, a pewter chalice with mermen-shaped handles, combs, toothbrushes, a floppy woolen Monmouth cap, a leather slipper with a green ribbon bow, several surgeons' instruments, including a brass tourniquet designed to help stop the flow of blood in extremities, and a pewter urethral syringe, used for injections against venereal disease, a small bottle of "rob," or lemon juice, essential for the prevention of scurvy, navigational instruments, twenty-five leather boots and shoes, a black-basalt tea service designed by Josiah Wedgwood, and an eighteen-karat-gold mourning ring inscribed with the words, "In Memory of my belov'd Brother, Capt. John Drew, drown'd 11 Jany. 1798, Aged 47," which had belonged to James Drew, whose brother John had drowned just four months before the *DeBraak* went down. But little treasure emerged and, save for a jaw and a metatarsus brought up by accident, no bones: The divers had been instructed to toss aside all skeletons and skulls.

Of the ship itself, only the starboard side of the hull, buried in mud, had survived the onslaught of worms, oxidation, and currents. This they raised in darkness with a thunderstorm brewing on the night of August 11, 1986. Dozens of boats clustered in a semicircle around the salvage barge as a huge crane lifted the hull out of the depths and into the glare of spotlights. At the eleventh hour, the salvagers chose not to use a fifteen-ton cradle custom-made for the pick, but used cables instead, and the hull slipped, spilling much of its contents back into the sea.

Once the ship was raised it lost its mythic status. Still, there are those who believe the treasure was lost in that careless moment, sunk deep again in murky waters, and may turn up somewhere on shore.

Here inside the elbow of the cape I can smell spring, not the loamy musk of woodland springs, but the warm tidal breath of the flats. Up and down the bayshore horseshoe crabs are gathered in masses, hundreds of them, some resting upside-down on their helmetlike shells, tails erect, claws waving, as though some kind of curious meeting were going on. I pick one up by the edge of its carapace, burnished like wet cobblestone, turn it over, and send it on its way toward the water. I wonder if my hand has a smell, a predator's scent, detected by tiny hairs at the base of the crab's legs, which act as chemoreceptors, allowing the crab to "smell" its predators and prey. When sunlight streams into the vestigial ventral eyes of a flipped horseshoe crab, its heart rate accelerates, then plummets. It uses its long spiky tail as a lever to right itself, but judging from the number of rotting corpses, it seems an ineffective tool. I flip another, and another, in eagerness to further life against death, but the numbers are too great, and I finally give up, leaving them to wait for the second tide to rise, wash them loose, and spirit them away or lay them higher on the shore to bleach and dry among the algal wrack and swarming flies.

Limulus polyphemus is the crab's scientific name, *Limulus* meaning sidelong or a little askew, and *polyphemus* for the Greek cyclops, one of those monstrous forms of life that Zeus banished from the earth, and the only one he allowed to return. The crab actually has nine eyes, including two large tilty spots like the compound eyes of a dragonfly on the top of its carapace, two simple eyes facing forward by which it receives ultraviolet light from the moon, and five almost microscopic light-receptive vestigial organs on the underside. It is no crab at all, but a descendant from the ancient line of Merostomates, marine arachnids, and thus is more closely related to common garden spiders, scorpions, and ticks than to blue, Dungeness, or lady crabs. If I stoop down to take a closer look at the crab's underbelly, I can see that its body divides neatly into three segments, and its large book gills are leaved like the book lungs of terrestrial arachnids. It also lacks the antennae of true crabs and the elaborate mouthparts, shredding its prey instead with bristles at the base of its legs.

Limulus is built like a little tank, its shell tough and chitinous, its body able to withstand big swings in temperature and salinity. Three species live along the coast of Southeast Asia;

one lives here. Our North American variety survives in the icy waters of Bar Harbor, Maine, and in the balmy tropics southward to the Yucatán, but its center of population is the Delaware Bay.

Last night I came down to count the mating crabs as part of an annual census, having consulted my watch and a calendrical table of the tides to reach the shore at the peak of high spring tide. The crabs had performed this same trick, without benefit of timekeepers or tables. Earlier in the spring, buried in ocean sediments beneath sixty feet of water, they had sensed the moment for vernal migration to begin, tipped off by their own little biological chronometers and the longer hours of daylight. Right on cue, in synchrony with the syzygy, they crawled out of the deeps to mate and lay eggs on the shore of the bay.

The night's full moon was huge, a giant milky white eye that blanched the dunes and gave the bay a thin white skin. Within an hour of the turning high tide, the females began to crawl out of the bay. They dug into the sand just below the high-tide mark and deposited their eggs in shallow, scraped hollows in the sand. They carried strings of clambering, nuzzling males (clamped on to them with mitten front legs), which they dragged over the eggs to fertilize them. One large female lumbered about like a restless ark, towing two small males and carrying on her back a snail, two slipper shells, several barnacles, and a cluster of twenty-four blue mussels. She was big, a good twenty-two inches from head to tail, and probably old as horseshoe crabs go: Attached organisms are a sign of age.

I paced the shore, measuring ten-meter segments and counting out loud to the strange rhythmic creaking of carapaces. Each female lays thousands of eggs in several nests. Once fertilized, the crabs have two weeks to develop from egg

Mating horseshoe crabs

to hatchling before the sun, earth, and new moon line up to produce the little spring tide, and the hatchlings must push up out of the stifling sand to ride the receding waters into the bay. The hatchlings are tiny, about an eighth of an inch across, and resemble nothing so much as the ancient trilobites of Cambrian times.

Given the crush of coupling carapaces, it's hard to imagine that there's cause for concern about the health of horseshoe crab populations. But in fact the numbers are not what they used to be. In the 1920s and '30s, five million horseshoe crabs were collected each year for garden fertilizer. They were stacked like cordwood on the beach and left to bake in the sun, then dried and coarsely ground into meal. After the numbers of spawning crabs plummeted in the 1960s, these mass harvestings stopped. The population has been rebuilding since then, but only slowly. The beaches the crabs use for spawning are going the way of bulkheads and groins, and the crabs themselves are still taken for eel and conch bait. They're also collected for a compound in their blue, copper-based blood—a clotting agent used to check drugs for the presence of bacteria—but these crabs are usually released alive after they're bled.

Out here with the moon and the black waters awash in sperm and eggs, the world seemed to shrink to the intimate clacking of shells. When I next looked up a bright halo of impending weather had exploded around the moon. From the foghorn came a lowing moan. Between eerie flashes of lightning the dark seemed to suck out all light. I had only a small flashlight in my pocket, which was useless in that black. I heard the hiss of rain; it was time to get out of the open. Another flash of lightning, the wind gusted, and the night roared.

This morning reveals the carnage, hundreds of crabs overturned in the act of mating by heavy waves. The sanderlings arrive first in loose scattered flocks, whistling and chipping in urgent hunger, to forage amidst the shells. But before long the flats are overrun with an unruly alphabet of birds: willets, turnstones, sandpipers, plovers, and dunlins scrabbling the sand and whirling up and down in tight agitated circles. When I tire of trying to differentiate the species, I go the other way: Peep becomes bird, bird becomes animal, animal, life, life, energy, which is easy in this swirl of wings and light. Or I imagine all of a bird's journeys, from cold scaley reptile to aery winged thing, from egg to embryo to adult, from south to north to south again.

These migratory shorebirds—which writer Peter Matthiessen calls "wind birds"—have a way of tying this little digit of coast to the far northern and southern reaches of the hemisphere. Among them is a plump, cinnamon-colored wader about the size of a robin. It is the red knot, *Calidris canutus rufus*, a species that summers in Tierra del Fuego, near the southern tip of South America, and breeds on islands of the central Canadian Arctic, where the high latitude offers longer hours of sunlight in which to feed chicks. Like most of the hordes, the red knot has flown thousands of miles nonstop to reach these flats.

Earlier in the spring, down there on the coasts of Tierra del Fuego, on the mud flats of Suriname and the desert beaches of Peru, the *Zugunruhe* had come, the restlessness of birds before migration. The first written record of the phenomenon may come from the prophet Jeremiah in the Old Testament: "The stork in the heaven knoweth her appointed times, and the turtle and the crane and the swallow observe the time of their coming." The quickening is sparked by a rhythmic internal timekeeper, a body clock. Wild passerines held captive in a room in their time of migration will become fretful and restless, hopping about, leaping from perch to perch, clustering on the south wall in autumn and the north wall in spring. The restlessness lasts for a time period proportional to the distance traveled by that species during its passage, even for birds who have never migrated.

The shorebirds leave their wintering grounds as evening descends and wing their way northward at night. How they are able to navigate so precisely even over the sea in the dark is still largely a mystery, though many migratory birds are thought to use a constellation of sensory cues, including sights, sounds, smells, and magnetic fields. At night, they're able to recognize the tilt and rotation of the sky and patterns of stars such as the Big Dipper, whose lip points toward the North Star. When celestial cues are lacking, they use an internal compass sensitive to the direction of the earth's magnetic field. The journeys of wind birds are prodigious. The sanderling and dunlin fly at fifty-five miles per hour for fifty hours nonstop, sometimes at elevations up to twenty thousand feet, where high winds toss them about. Some drop from fatigue, dying alone, as wild things do.

In contrast to the crab's migratory routine, the north–south journeys of shorebirds came about quite recently, perhaps in response to the ebb and flow of great ice sheets across the northern continents during the Pleistocene epoch. This was around the same time our species leapt what philosopher and paleontologist Pierre Teilhard de Chardin called the Threshold of Reflection: Something in humanity "turned back on itself and so to speak took an infinite leap forward. Outwardly, almost nothing in the organs had changed. But in depth, a great revolution had taken place: consciousness was now leaping and boiling." Which may help to explain why we rustle somewhere deep in spring and fall and feel an affinity for birds on their journeys.

Unlike many species of migratory birds, the wind birds don't migrate along a broad front, but funnel through a few key spots with a concentrated food source. Because of its population of breeding horseshoe crabs, the Delaware Bay is the largest staging site for northbound migratory shorebirds in eastern North America, a critical stepping-stone along a hemispheric pathway that reaches from the windswept shores of Austral South America to the high tundra of the Arctic. To supply enough energy for the direct two-thousand-mile flight to breeding grounds, the birds gorge on the horseshoe crab eggs during their stay here, squabbling and jabbing aggressively at the shallow pits to get their fill. In a period of two or three weeks, each bird increases its weight by 40 percent or more. Sanderlings double their weight by ingesting an average

Shorebirds feeding on horseshoe crab eggs

of nine thousand eggs a day. Three-quarters of the *rufa* race of red knots passes through here, and half of all the New World's ruddy turnstones and Atlantic sanderlings. The latter alone consume close to six billion eggs each season, about twenty-seven tons.

I poke at a hole and wonder whether this clutch of sweet eggs will go into a bronze hide or a thing with wings. I'm struck by the number of these tiny pearly green pellets that fail to find passage into light. Apart from the red knots, ruddy turnstones, and sanderlings, eight other species of shorebirds eat horseshoe crab eggs, along with sparrows, mourning doves, cowbirds, common grackles, pigeons, and three kinds of gulls. Turtles prey on them, and mice; so does the raccoon, who steals down through the dune grass to dig them up. Eggs caught in the receding waters of the tide are snatched up by crabs, eel, and minnows. Mollusks scavenge those that drop to the bottom. Nematode worms parasitize the egg clusters. The loss is enormous, but somehow they keep ahead of the slaughter. Each spring the beach is crawling with the successful.

It's an old story. I've read in several respectable sources that horseshoe crabs are "living fossils." Strictly speaking, they are not. Our American species has no fossil record at all; it ranges back only twenty million years, to the Miocene epoch. But fossils chipped from rocks in the Alps show that ancestors of horseshoe crabs—dozens of different kinds of them—were scraping about in the Triassic Period, over two hundred million years ago. The differences between those fossil ancestors and the four species of horseshoe crabs that exist today are slight. So, something like this crab has endured for eons despite an ineffectual tool for righting itself when flipped in the heat of mating. It has survived not only predators, but all the planet's chameleonlike changes—the births and deaths of mountains, of shores on unremembered seas—as well as whatever disaster brought about the demise of dinosaurs and countless other creatures more fantastic and complex. For this reason, it has a special fascination for me, along with other strange creatures that have outlasted most living things: the coelocanth, the deep sea mussel, the cockroach, which has endured in unwinking abundance since Carboniferous times three hundred million years ago.

In speculating on the nature of angels' time, St. Thomas Aquinas spoke of the duration of human souls and other divine beings as somewhere midway between time and eternity, having a beginning but no end. This notion might hold for the way horseshoe crabs occupy time, these creatures so durable that they antedate most other life forms, so adaptable that their survival as a species may, for all we know, approach eternity.

I wonder if our general fascination with long-lived creatures isn't at some level a vote against the possibility that our own species isn't long for this world. Most of the time we think of ourselves as ageless and timeless (which may explain why we reach for the permanent beauty of a perfect whelk, for bottles from a dead ship, but toss aside the bones). Because of the way we have evolved, our minds move easily backward and forward only two generations ahead and two behind. It takes a bull's-eye in time like the horseshoe crab to hurl the mind beyond these bounds and force the long view. Like marine fossils found on mountaintops, the crabs give a cold splash of geologic perspective.

Here's another take on long time. I read recently that Earth's spin is slowing through time, about one fifty-thousandth of a second per year. As long ago as the eighteenth century, Immanuel Kant suggested the reason: tidal friction. The tide sloshing around the globe creates friction that acts as a brake on Earth's rotation. And because a law called conservation of angular momentum is at work in the Earth–moon system, the moon compensates for this slowing by moving away from Earth about an inch each year. If the full moon looked big last night, I wonder what it looked like to the ancestors of horseshoe crabs who lived in Triassic seas hundreds of millions of years ago. It is this kind of news that makes me want to rush out into the dark to witness an ancient ritual, a tiny segment of evolutionary time, one spring in twenty thousand thousand springs.

Five

Fathoms

$\mathcal{C}$rabs again. Real crabs this time, *Ocypode qua-drata*, the swift-footed ghost crab, abundant from Cape Henlopen to Brazil and hunter of night beaches. I've come down to the cape at sunset on an early summer day. The only sounds are those of crickets buzzing in the beach grass and the regular slap of waves. The sun, a ball of fire, sinks and is swallowed by a bank of clouds long before it reaches the horizon. The light warms and red-dens. A flock of gulls lets me come very close be-fore they send up an explosion of white wings. They circle about and a few seconds later, settle again behind me, a quarrelsome knot of dim shad-ows picking through the sea scraps. A squadron of cormorants passes low against the reflected af-terlight. The waters darken. For a brief moment Venus shines alone, then stars fill the night.

I flip on my light and startle a ghost crab. It's a good size, two and a half inches of furious activ-ity against the pale sand. I've watched smaller members of its tribe, sidling from dune to sea, halting to dig for mole crabs, then dashing madly back, their camouflage so effective they look like bits of wind-shifted sand or detritus. Their exquisite protective disguise arises from pigmented cells called chromatophores. The pigment migrates in response to light and temperature, causing color changes that help the crab mimic its surroundings.

This one scuttles sideways on the tips of eight legs. When I press in, it raises the last pair of legs off the ground and accelerates, disappearing down a hole at the toe of the foredunes. I flash my light in the opening, but to no avail. The burrow may shoot or spiral down to depths of five or six feet. One morning I saw an adult crab emerge popeyed from a burrow beneath the awning of a horseshoe crab shell, cradling a load of sand in its legs. It paused for a moment, then flung its load down and flashed back into the hole. It was some time later before it reemerged with another load.

Ghost crabs breathe air through narrow, slitlike openings between their third and fourth legs and can live for long periods out of water, but their gills must be kept moist in order to function. At intervals they visit the swash zone to replenish the moisture. Theirs is an evolutionary drama, says Rachel Carson, the coming to land of a sea creature. The larvae begin life as part of the plankton drifting in the open ocean. They become amphibious as they grow, at some point following an urge to pop through the water membrane into the throttling air. They come ashore a rolled-up, fistlike ball of legs and torso, protected from the bruising surf by a tough cuticle. Small immature crabs burrow near the water, just above high-tide line. As they mature, the crabs become more and more independent of the sea, foraging as much as a quarter of a mile inland. Still, they must return to the wash of broken surf to wet their gills and release their eggs.

Ghost crab in burrow

In their bondage to the sea, ghost crabs resemble their sometime prey, a tiny creature only a half inch in length that leaps about the light of my lamp when I set it on the sand. Beach fleas explode into the air with an agile flexing of legs. Not fleas at all, but crustaceans with flealike powers of jumping, they hop distances of more than fifty times their own length using three pairs of short, stiff rear legs. The fleas also bear three abdominal legs modified for swimming. They, too, hover between land and sea, still possessing gills, though much reduced in size from those of their marine ancestors.

A beach flea lives close to the wrack line, burrowing in the moist sand beneath drift seaweed in the heat of day to avoid desiccating its gills and body and emerging only at night to browse on bits of decaying plant and animal matter. Using the moon and other celestial cues to guide it, the flea moves up and down the beach with the tides, staying within a narrow ribbon of damp sand. It shares with the ghost crab a fear of the full tide. Both crab and flea will drown if kept under water for any period of time, as we ourselves might drown.

I switch off my lamp. A pale moon has risen, spreading its diffuse light across the water's surface. Small waves shower light foam on the shore. Otherwise the night is black. It was 350 million years ago that the first pioneer of land life heaved itself out of the sea: an arthropod, one of the great phyla that later gave rise to crabs and insects, a stumbling, adventurous refugee that lived the strange half-aquatic, half-terrestrial life of the ghost crab and beach flea. The small scuttlings at my feet presage the future, pointing out that life is not fixed like a butterfly pinned on a board, but still brewing, groping on in countless directions.

One hot morning in late June, I set off in a Boston whaler with friends to look for pelagic birds. I sit in the front of the boat where the jolts are hard, bouncing along toward the open blue, the sea disappearing as we mount a rise, then reappearing as we smack down hard. The coast recedes to a thin featureless crust, then disappears altogether. It takes most of the morning to reach Five Fathoms, a fishing spot forty miles out to sea. Alone with our boat, we cut the motor and drift, binoculars trained on the horizon. Not a pelagic bird in sight. A gull swaying gently overhead cocks its head as if to ask what we are doing way out here in such a duckling of a boat.

Our whaler carries some sophisticated electronic naviga-tion equipment, but I can't help wondering what would happen if it failed, along with our motor, and the weather turned bad. Sea nomads in the archipelagoes of Southeast Asia can look up at the sun and clouds, look down at the sea, and accurately read both time and their whereabouts. But for most of us, the open ocean seems mute and lonely when you're out there in the middle of it. A report I read in *The Journal of Navigation* suggested that humans have an innate sense of direction. Laboratory experiments showed that people's ability to pinpoint North gradually improved after multiple challenges. "Orientation in humans is a latent sense," said the researchers, though in most of us it seems to have disappeared from lack of use.

I don't know how long we sit. The sun beats down, and the water calms to a sheet of thick, undulating metal. Suddenly, twenty yards from our tiny craft, a great slick-backed blue mass lifts in a rising swell and rolls forward, flashing a sharp hook of fin and a bright turquoise patch. It disappears, then rises again, slow, cloudlike, and blows a jet of white vapor ten feet high, like an upside-down pyramid.

It is a finback whale, the second largest baleen whale after the blue, and Earth's only asymmetrically colored mammal. The left side of its head and jaw is dark, the right side light. The purpose of this asymmetrical pigmentation remains a mystery, although it may be an adaptation for the capture of small schooling fish such as herring. The whale swims around the fish to the right in smaller and smaller circles, showing only its translucent, invisible white side so as not to startle its prey. As the herring clump together, the whale turns into the pack, mouth open, and gobbles them up, its pleated throat bulging, expanding bellowlike to take in the liquid meal. Then it presses the water out of the baleen plates that grow down from its upper gums and swallows what's left behind.

Our boat bobs about in the waves above Five Fathoms. We each face a different direction to cover the scope of ocean, but the giant beast has disappeared. Finbacks can swim underwater for forty minutes without drawing breath. Like other whales, their ancestors were four-legged land animals that hunted in the tidal shallows around river deltas and the edges of the warm, shallow seas. Sometime around fifty or sixty million years ago, they abandoned land life for the ocean, perhaps following their prey farther and farther out to sea. Paleontologists digging in Pakistan recently unearthed the remains of an ancient whale with legs and long feet like a seal, a missing link in the evolutionary chain. The scientists called the animal *Ambulocetus natans,* "the walking whale that swam."

Over the course of millions of years, these creatures slipped protean through many shapes, losing their legs and pelvises and developing a horizontal fluked tail to propel them through the seas. Their bodies eventually assumed a smooth, hairless form perfectly suited to swimming and swept back for speed. Their forelimbs grew into organs for steering and balancing in a liquid environment. Sound became their light and hearing their vision. Deep within the fifty-ton body of a finback is born a pure, radiant booming an octave deeper than the lowest note on a piano. Such sound waves can travel enormous distances in the sea. Trapped in the deep sound channel, a layer of water where sound waves bend back on themselves and retain their energy, whale sounds can carry several hundred miles.

Both whales and dolphins bear traces of their kinship to land creatures. Their flippers have bones similar to those in a human arm and hand, though much reshaped. Whales often retain tiny leg bones. Dolphins catch the same diseases as pigs and cattle. In a throwback to a dim past, dolphins along the coast of the Carolinas briefly revisit the world of their ancestors, having learned once again to feed at low tide on the edge of the land, herding schools of fish toward the mud flats, riding the waves in, and plucking the fish from the shore.

Once, on a visit to a whaling ship, biologist Victor Scheffer acquired a whale fetus only four inches long. "I took the little creature, packed in ice cubes, to the mainland," he wrote. "At my hotel I bought a pint of vodka and a bottle of shaving lotion. I mixed these in a washbasin, slit the belly and chest of the fetus with a razor blade, and embalmed it overnight in the fragrant solution. Later I dissected it in my laboratory. . . . In profile, the little head could . . . have belonged to an infant pig, with eyes shut, lower jaw protruding beyond the snout, and nostrils at the front. . . . The penis protruded; the rudimentary nipples were evident; even the ears were there—tiny ridges of skin, most unfitting for a whale. There were actually traces of whiskers, casting a long shadow from an ancestor dead now forty million years."

In the course of development, embryonic whales grow rudimentary legs, nostrils, and surface genitals. Then the hindlimbs disappear, the nostrils slide backward to become blowholes, the genitals vanish inside a slit. In the fetus of a finback whale, tooth germs appear in the gums, but by the time the fetus has reached a length of thirteen feet, they have vanished.

I once saw a jar containing a pickled human embryo in the National Museum of Natural History. It had a bulging reptilian head, a tail, and arches like gills just beneath the head.

Finback whale

Our own living organs, eyes, backbones, hands, and feet originated in far places and different eras of time. Four hundred million years ago our piscine forebears wiggled over muddy flats, throwing their bodies in an S-curve. As a consequence, our arms swing in opposition to the swing of our legs. Our reflected past and some shadow of the future is paradoxically written in our bodies. We, too, are changelings, made of millions of bits of information strung together from an odd little alphabet and brought into being by an astronomical number of chance events over the long course of evolution. But for this we might be hovering just above the warm mud. As Stephen Jay Gould has written, those stubby, sluggish fins that became weight-bearing limbs—the necessary prerequisite to terrestrial life—evolved in an uncommon group of fishes off the main line. They were a fluke.

   In some way all creatures bear traces of their past: ghost crabs their gills, whales their vestigial limbs, humans our liquid cells, the salt water running in our veins, our feeling for the sea. "Why upon your first voyage as a passenger," wrote Melville, "did you yourself feel such a mystical vibration when first told that you and your ship were out of sight of land?"

In most other animals . . . the eyes are so planted as imperceptibly to blend their visual power, so as to produce one picture and not two to the brain; the peculiar position of the whale's eyes, effectually divided as they are by many cubic feet of solid head, which towers between them like a great mountain separating two lakes in valleys; this, of course, must wholly separate the impressions which each independent organ imparts. The whale, therefore, must see one distinct picture on this side, and another distinct picture on that side; while all between must be profound darkness and nothingness to him. . . . Is his brain so much more comprehensive, combining, and subtle than man's, that he can at the same moment of time attentively examine two distinct prospects, one on one side of him, and the other in an exactly opposite direction?

—*Herman Melville*

The

Great

Marsh

The Great Marsh is a broad plain of mud and grass that lies a mile northwest of Lewes. It's roughly rectangular, five square miles, bordered on three sides by uplands and on the fourth, by Beach Plum Island. Along the southern border Oyster Rocks Neck and Hells Neck run a half mile or so into the marsh, their wooded uplands reaching an elevation of about ten feet. A few islands, or hummocks, rise out of the sea of grass and support little forests of pine and cedar, sassafras, red maple, and black gum. Otherwise, this is a landscape of no relief, flat and featureless. The major tool for navigating here is the system of tortuous streams that crease the grassy plain: Canary Creek, Fisher Creek, Black Hog Gut, and Old Mill Creek, which meanders in giant loopy S-curves from Red Mill Pond to the Broadkill River and drains nearly three-quarters of the marsh. The Delaware Bay flows dendritically through Old Mill Creek and its tributaries. The creeks predate the marsh, which was born seven thousand years ago when the rapidly rising sea drowned a valley of the Broadkill River, transforming it into a small lagoon. Silt gradually clogged the lagoon and filled it, then pioneering grasses advanced over the mud, trapping soil in the tiny baffles of their roots and anchoring it to make marsh.

Great Marsh from Canary Creek

Just before sunrise, low tide. I walk out into the marsh in the dark, stepping around chocolate brown pools agitated with the scratching and scuttling of fiddler crabs, past delicate marsh pinks, absent their color in the white-wash light. Waves of warm air waft up from the mudbanks bared by the outcreeping tide, a strong sulphur smell, not unpleasant. The beam of my flashlight catches the giant ghostly pale blossoms of the seashore mallow, *Kosteletzkya virginica.* I linger here for a moment, hoping to "shine" the eyes of a wolf spider, a species with mirrorlike membranes that reflect light.

The darkness of the marsh is not the close darkness of woods, where blackness pours up from between the trees, but a thin, liquid, open, far-reaching darkness that descends onto the grass. Silence stretches from horizon to horizon, broken only by the occasional call of a whippoorwill, a sound that carries easily over the flat topography, somehow amplified by the open acres of air and the drum-flat surface of the nearby bay.

My destination is a small tower of metal scaffolding fifteen feet high topped by a wooden blind that sits about a mile into the marsh. The path to the tower is wandering and uncertain and moves erratically between firm ground and sloppy bottom that sucks hungrily at my hipwaders. Even in the night damp I'm sweating profusely, bundled against mosquitoes in long pants and a flannel shirt. Beneath the grass is a deep black brew of river silt and clay trapped over millennia, bottomed twenty feet down by hard-packed yellow sand. Every fifteen steps or so I sink deep in a soft oozy hole. When I reach the tower, I peel off my damp shirt and my hipwaders, coated with a glossy mud sheen, and sit in my socks.

The sky above the Great Marsh is so broad that it hosts more than one celestial event. This morning a sagging August moon a day or two past full is setting in the west, and in the east, a tomato of a sun is edging up over the horizon. Soon it's swallowed up by a reef of purple clouds, casting the marsh in monochromatic light. The tower's open, rickety, crow's-nest platform offers a 360-degree view of the low country around it. I can just make out the lean profile of a great blue heron well camouflaged by stillness. It plunges its head into a pool and comes up with a fish, swallows it, and then raises itself slowly with deep parenthetical beats of its huge wings. I can hear the cackle of a green heron, but can't pick it out of the ranks of green roughage.

For months after I arrived here, I did not understand the draw of this leveled, subdued landscape, couldn't focus on any one part of it long enough to penetrate its surface. This summer I spent time in the tower with a young scientist from the Delaware Division of Fish and Wildlife. Randy Cole is a native of this place who was raised on duck hunting and wears his hipwaders like a second skin. He is studying the wildlife drawn to several artificial ponds dug into the marsh a few seasons before. The ponds are part of a state program designed to control mosquitoes and at the same time, draw back some of the wildlife that has been chivied out by earlier mosquito control efforts. In the 1930s state officials had a complex system of crisscrossing ditches cut into the marsh, not with the loops and curves of natural creeks, but with the straight lines and right angles of the planning grid. In so doing they broke the natural order of the marsh, disturbed a rhythm old and of vast importance. The grid-ditching drained the big natural ponds whose permanent waters once attracted breeding colonies of black ducks and gadwall. The new ponds, a dozen half-acre pools contoured for natural effect, are designed to bring the birds back.

Randy's job is to record the species and number of animals that use the ponds for feeding or breeding. While we sit and watch for waterfowl, he points out salient marsh plants: *Spartina alterniflora*, or smooth cordgrass; saltmeadow hay; sea lavender; spike grass; and *Salicornia*, or saltwort. The latter is an odd little thing with leaves like long swollen toes, the only plant that can survive the extreme salinity found in the salt pans that pockmark the higher marsh, where water has been concentrated by evaporation until its salt content is several times that of the sea. At this time of year its spears are turning red from the roots up, giving it the look of a bizarre Christmas ornament made of flesh.

The marsh vegetation, which to my first bewildered surveys was utterly indistinct, has slowly sorted itself into recognizable zones, not altogether different from a mountain's, where leafy deciduous woodland gives way to pines, and then to treeless tundra, only here the distinction between zones comes down to shifts of inches. In the marsh's higher reaches—the hummocks and along the landward edges, out of reach of all but the highest spring or storm tides—grow two woody plants collectively called saltbush. There's marsh elder, *Iva frutescens*, an awkward stalky shrub with thick, fleshy leaves, and *Baccharis halimifolia*, the groundsel tree. Now in late summer, its seedheads look like hundreds of tiny white plumes. Below, but still wetted only twice a month by spring tides, grows salt-meadow hay, windrows of fine light stalks that swirl and mat in giant cowlicks. Lower still, by only two inches or so, salt-meadow hay gives way to the big, coarse, dark green stalks of *Spartina alterniflora*, which are flooded by every tide. *Spartina* is remarkable for its rich ability to solicit sunlight and its ingenious adaptations to the salt flood that sweeps through the marsh twice daily. Close to a million cubic feet of brackish water flow in during flood tide, nearly doubling the water's salt content. Salt sucks water from living cells. But by special cunning *Spartina* can drink the water while excluding the salt: membranes on the plant's roots pull the freshwater from the sea. What little salt makes its way into the sap is excreted by glands in the plant's leaves. At low tide you can see the exiled salt crystals flashing in the sun.

On the walk out to the tower, Randy would squat down to show me the miniature tropical forest amid the thick stems of *Spartina*, a hot, humid, nearly windless environment. On and around the stems grows a microscopic, polycultural jungle of hundreds of species of diatoms, algae, and dinoflagellates, which trap phosphorus, nitrates, and other elements vital to marsh life. Beneath it all, the marsh mud is black, blacker than the soil of the Mississippi Delta, and richer. Each autumn the aerial stems of *Spartina* die, bend down, break, mix into the black muck. Bacteria decompose the leaves, breaking them into small particles, detritus, which the tide spreads across the marsh surface, providing a pasture of food. An astronomer friend of mine saw this instantly when he looked down on the mud: "This place is *trashed* with life."

Pull up the blanket of marsh, give it a shake, and out would tumble coffee-bean snails, *Melampus bidentatus*, little half-inch creatures tinted with brown and green, as well as grass-hoppers, beetles, ants, flies, and cinch bugs, which feed on *Spartina*'s tender leaves, and plant hoppers, which suck its juices. Also fiddler crabs and mud crabs, oysters and dense clumps of ribbed mussels, which pave the mud along the creeks where the tide floods regularly. According to one study, this marsh supports more than three and a half million mussels per acre. Out, too, would tumble diamondback terrapins, turtles the size of a small skull, their segmented pentagons fused to form a leathery dome, their reptilian heads spotted like a leopard. The diamondback was once here in great numbers, but its sweet flesh made it a gastronomic delicacy and the target of tireless collectors.

The shake wouldn't loose such tenacious insiders as the larva of the common marsh fly, family *Chloropidae*, which lives in the stems of *Spartina* and eats the plant's tissue. (The adults are so small, only two or three millimeters long, that they are nearly invisible except when swarming.) Nor would it dislodge the larvae of the fierce-biting greenhead fly, whose singular appetites are described by John and Mildred Teal in *Life and Death of the Salt Marsh*. "The larvae are maggots, soft, elongate, leathery-skinned, lumpy individuals with a pair of organs for breathing air at one end and a pair of sharp jaws at the other. They wriggle through the mud eating anything they come across, including others of their kind. If a number of *Tabanus* maggots are put together in a dish, the end result is one fat, temporarily contented individual."

Here are some of the thirty or so species of fish that swim the waters of the Great Marsh: the small, glistening fish known as silversides, the four-spined stickleback, anchovy, northern pipefish, two kinds of herring, young striped bass, sea robins, summer flounder, naked gobies, striped mullet and white perch, eel, croaker, menhaden, northern kingfish, and three species of killifish, including the mummichog, a name that comes from a Narraganset word meaning "they go in great numbers."

The sun has reappeared above the cloud reef, a second bloom. In this low morning light the marsh looks different than it does under cloud cover or high sun, not a hazy watercolor wash, but a dazzling mosaic of distinctly different greens. The tide is sliding up the marsh slope, slithering into the creeks and spilling over between the blades of grass. The up, down, in, out of the tides makes this place dangerous—sometimes inundating animals with lethal doses of saltwater, sometimes exposing them to a devastating high-and-dry death—but also inconceivably rich. The tides distribute food and flush out waste, encouraging rapid growth and quick decay. Adaptation to this pulse is the contract that all successful marsh creatures have signed with a country half land, half sea. When the ebbing tide bares the flats, hundreds of scraping chitinous legs and claws scribe the mud as fiddler crabs emerge from their burrows to search for bacteria, fungi, minute algae, and fermenting marsh plants. Tiny star-shaped pigment cells dotting the crab's body obey the compounded rhythms of sun and tide. The cells contain granules of dark pigment, which dis-

ghost crab ? perse at daytime low tide, giving the crabs the color of the mudbank and thus protecting them from predators. At night the pigment granules shrink from the cell's reaches and cluster together, the color fades, and the crabs turn the pale ivory-white of moonlight. These changes occur every day at a different hour, synchronized with the tides.

Now, as the salt tide seeps up the mudbank, the fiddlers are waiting until the water reaches their knees before they disappear into their deep mud tunnels to wait out the deluge. Though they breathe air with a primitive lung beneath the edge of their shell, they can hole up in their burrows with no oxygen for long periods—for months in cold water—a feat that makes the limit of our own tolerance for organic variation seem narrow indeed. A few moments' loss of oxygen and we rapidly descend into unconsciousness.

Coffee-bean snails, too, are air-breathers, but they go up rather than down when the tide rises. Like ghost crabs and beach fleas, they are members of a race that is learning to live outside the sea. Somehow they anticipate rising tides, creeping up the stalks of grass well before the water arrives. They take a breath of air that will hold them for an hour or so if the drowning sea submerges them.

Spiders and insects such as grasshoppers keep company with the snail, scaling stems to escape the high tide. This habit exposes the climbers to the keen eyes and hungry beaks of birds. The Teals once described the scene of an especially high tide, insects hopping, jumping, and flying onto taller plants until "only the tallest grasses along the creeks mark the meandering channels and these grasses are weighted and bending at the tips, alive with insects. Sparrows and wrens from the marsh, buntings and warblers from the land, gulls and terns from the beach, and swallows, dip, fly, settle, and swim along the twist-

ing lanes of helpless insects and gorge themselves." I've seen
swallows swooping over the marsh, snatching insects from
mid-air, then suddenly dodging a marsh hawk's hook and talon
in a startling turnabout of predator and prey.

Sunlight to marsh grass to grasshopper to swallow to
hawk: these are some of the links that compose the marsh web.
Learning a place is like this, glimpsing the individuals, the pinpoint touches of color on the broad canvas, randomly splattered. You pick them out, sort them out, name them, then
tumble them back into the landscape, and by reading and more
observation, figure out how they fit together. As more spaces
are filled in, the image or weave is revealed, the continuous
meshing intimacy. It helps to have a native tutor, and a sense
of the storyline, the narrative over time. In the marsh, the little
rhythms of the day have a way of focusing attention on particular species, the way the slow, small meter of an Emily Dickinson poem brings each syllable into close-up. *poetry* <

Noon, high tide. The marsh is a flat, dazzling mirror anchored by
green studs. The high sun has robbed it of the play of shifting
light in which it luxuriated this morning, brought it silently to
whiteness. It looks uninhabited, and yet I know that each square
inch of mud is crowded with twitchers, alive with drama,
tragedy, plot and adventure, fierce eating and being eaten.

The mosquitoes have left me alone this morning, but
once the sun goes down, I'll hear what D. H. Lawrence called
that "small, high, hateful bugle in my ear." Huge swarms of
mosquitoes used to range over this region, bands of millions
moving in unison, several feet thick and hundreds of feet wide,
their frenzied wingbeats producing a single, singing hum. In
1788 an observer at Cape Henlopen wrote:

The people are afflicted with a eveil, not much unlike, and almost as severe as, some of the plagues of Egypt. I mean the inconceivable swarms of muscatoes and sandflies which infest every place, and equally interrupt the tranquility of the night and the happiness of the day. Their attacks are intolerable upon man as well as beast. The poor cows and horses in order to escape from these tormentors stand whole days in ponds of water with only their heads exposed.

Delaware is home to fifty-three species of mosquitoes—with names like *Aedes excrucians, Coquilletiddia perturbans, A. tormentor,* and *A. vexans*—each adapted to occupy a particular niche. The high marsh saltmeadow hay around here suits *A. sollicitans,* the salt-marsh mosquito. Females of the species lay their eggs in the moist mud of potholes found in and around the tufts of salt hay, which are flooded only infrequently. When spring tides or storm tides or rainfall fill the potholes, the eggs quickly hatch. The larvae rest just under the surface of the pool, breathing through little snorkel-like air tubes and feeding on microscopic organisms. On their way to adulthood they pass through four larval stages and a pupal phase, a metamorphosis that in warm weather can take less than ten days. When the adults emerge, they mate over the marsh. Then the females set out to search for a blood meal.

In the early 1930s a man could make a dollar a day digging ditches for the Delaware Mosquito Control Commission. The answer to the problem of the salt-marsh mosquito, the state believed, lay in disrupting the insect's life cycle by draining off the small shallow ponds of water that served as breeding pools. With this in mind, managers placed a grid of dots over maps of Delaware's marshes and then connected the dots with a ruler. These straight lines would become ditches hand-dug, twenty inches wide, twenty inches deep, one hundred and fifty feet apart, that would drain all marshes, high and low, whether or not they were suitable breeding grounds for mosquitoes. To help with the project, the federal government assigned four companies from the Civilian Conservation Corps, eight hundred men. One company set up camp in Lewes in a big building on Savannah Road topped by a brass and copper weathervane in the shape of a giant mosquito.

The ditch digging was slow, hard work, but the operation was conducted with military efficiency. In four years the Corps had installed eleven and a half million linear feet of ditches across forty-four thousand acres of Delaware, including virtually all of the salt marsh in the southeastern part of the state.

Every time they dug one of those ditches, it was like pulling the plug from a bathtub. The full effects are only now being uncovered. The rookeries of breeding waterfowl and other birds have shrunk or disappeared for want of pools in which to feed. Where the ditching changed water levels, that tall, tassel-fringed reed, *Phragmites australis*, spread across the marsh, crowding out the marsh grasses so essential to the food web. In some places, the drainage ditches opened areas of marsh to more frequent flooding at lower tide levels. Less organic debris accumulated on marsh surfaces and populations of invertebrates at the base of the marsh food web crashed. Ironically, the small pools that formed behind the mounds of spoil created new breeding grounds for *A. sollicitans*.

The orderly ousting of the low, wet lands along this coast is not a new thing. For hundreds of years, people have considered these worlds miasmic, breeding grounds of choking vapors, of "exhalations [that] produced ague and intermittent fevers in the autumn and plursies in the spring," said an 1838 edition of the *Delaware Register and Farmers' Magazine*. The only good marsh was a drained marsh. Beginning in the seventeenth century, the Dutch—those masters of land drainage in Europe—and their colonial successors ditched and diked the mirey edges of the New World to create farmland and the squared geometry of our coastal towns. In the 1780s Delaware had 480,000 acres of marshes and swamps. In the 1990s only half of that remains.

nice

Late afternoon pivots into dusk. The tide has begun to recede without my noticing, the eddying currents carrying out the rich detritus from decayed *Spartina* that will feed the hordes of tiny planktonic animals that are themselves food for the greater creatures of the bay and sea.

One proposed solution to the destruction of wetlands is mitigation or "no net loss." The idea is this: Anyone who destroys a wetland must create one of similar size somewhere else. Plant some grass, introduce some keystone species, and hope that these serve as a sort of gravitational force that will draw in the myriad elements of the marsh community. But no new marsh can recreate the complex chemistry of mud cooked over millennia, the dying down of *Spartina* in the cool of a thousand autumns, the slow, steady mixing of bacteria and algae. Nor can it guarantee the proper assembly of species, birds, insects, plants, bacteria, each occupying a precise niche and locked in intimate relationships. The created marsh may look like a marsh to the casual eye, the eye of the passerby. Perhaps in some measure it acts like one. But it is not the real thing. Is it enough to make replicas, perfectly intelligible and diminished?

Sunset, low tide. The mosquitoes have finally found me, tipped off by the hot chemical breath of my skin. They are odd sorts of carnivores. "The lady whines, then dines; is slapped and killed," says poet Brad Leithauser, "yet it's her killer's blood that has been spilled." It is true that only the female pursues a blood meal: the male sticks to nectar. Only she has the long, stabbing mouthparts that penetrate skin. These form a flexible tube with serrations that neatly slice my skin tissue and a curved tip that scans for blood just beneath the skin's surface. When the mosquito finds a capillary, she draws the blood up through the tube with two sturdy pumps in her head. At the same time, she sends saliva back down another hollow tube. The saliva, which inhibits the clotting of my blood, causes the irritating itching and swelling. It can also carry disease. When Thomas Nuttall traveled across the country almost two hundred years ago, he took with him a one-celled parasite of the genus *Plasmodium*, which he had picked up from an *Anopheles* mosquito he met in a Delaware swamp. During most of his remaining years, he suffered malarial attacks.

Those wading birds on the ponds below are my partners in torment. Mosquitoes find their bills and eyes, the flesh peeking through their thin head feathers, their long exposed legs. A hunting green heron will let biting mosquitoes cover its legs and head before it will twitch or flutter and lose its prey. Our blood provides the female mosquito with the protein she needs to produce a new generation. She'll suck up to four times her own weight at a single sitting, about a millionth of a gallon, which she stores in her inner abdomen. (A two-bit tour of the insect would have to pause at this organ, unfettered by appendages and therefore able to distend enormously to house blood.) Her swelling gut triggers the secretion of hormones that prompt her eggs to mature. One blood meal provides enough nutrition to produce up to two hundred eggs. Without it, she can lay only a dozen eggs or so. You have to admire the power packed into her humming body. One ten-thousandth of

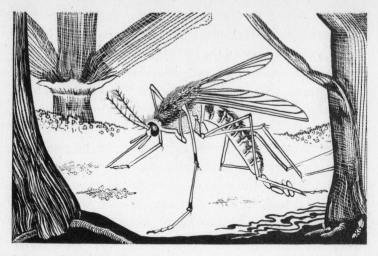

Salt-marsh mosquito laying eggs

an ounce and a brain only slightly bigger than the period at the end of this sentence. Her wings hum at two hundred to five hundred beats per second and will carry her up to fifty miles from her brood marsh in search of a blood meal. She can lay a new batch of eggs every two weeks, and may lay as many as three or four batches of eggs during her summer of existence.

Aldo Leopold says that the beauty of marshes doesn't scream at you; it has a slow, lyrical welling effect. Likewise, the deterioration beneath its green ranks only gradually discloses itself, and only to the knowing eye. One woman here knows the marsh well, sees it intimately like the house of her childhood, now skewed and malfunctioning, with termite-eaten floorboards, frayed wiring, rotting beams. She fights hard to save it, with some success: Her detractors call her the wicked witch of the wetlands. I've seen her at meetings with officials deciding the fate of one piece of drowned country after another. She knits while she listens, her needles flashing and clicking harder and faster as her rage mounts, and I wonder whether those pale pink sweaters and booties don't contain the names of the bureaucrats and businessmen who would do in our marshlands.

Randy Cole sees it, too, sees the body with skin intact but bones broken. Gone are the great pools of open water that once covered forty acres of the Great Marsh, pools that were nearly always full, replenished twice in twenty-four hours by tidal streams from the great sea, twice left brimming for crowds of rummaging, raucous ducks, their wings striking water again and again before they broke into the air. In recent seasons, Randy has found few breeding birds; the artificial ponds are not working the open water sorcery. The plaster falls from a mural; locusts consume a section of tapestry, taking with it some critical incidents. Consider the elements of any tale: Pull one out and the story changes. If John Donne is right, any death diminishes the whole, even the death of an obscure piece of damp ground. It is, in its way, a reservoir of old authority and a link to our own beginnings.

I swat as evening descends. In the low light there is a kind of intense clarity, a last assertion of detail. Then the light withdraws slowly, and the detail weakens, evaporates, bleeds away. The lines of grass dissolve; the hummocks lose their outline, then their form, gradually, almost imperceptibly. There is a graying, a blending, as everything becomes dim, incomprehensible. The first star is out, a white diamond in a sea of night sky.

quaking bog

The
Strange
and
Wonderful

$\mathcal{I}$ couldn't sleep last night. When I closed my eyes, flocks of exotic, fantastically colored birds drifted by, crimson, emerald, azure, floating through a garden of lush tropical vegetation. Some had long, streaming tail feathers like macaws or crests like cockatoos; others were quite improbable, speckled with luminescent green or adorned with blazing scarlet and yellow epaulets. It was like a vision produced by drugs and distinctly at odds with the sea air soughing through my bedroom screen.

It was the upshot of an evening spent thumbing through a book on parrots of the New World, an exercise prompted by a meeting in the wild with a flock of parakeets. The first time I saw the birds was one morning in early February when, acting on a tip from Bill Frech, I went looking for them at Silver Lake in downtown Rehoboth. It was one of those raw gray days. The temperature hovered around freezing, and a skin of ice had formed on the lake, forcing the geese to its periphery.

I love the slow murmur of beach towns this

time of year. Ragged flags flutter over battened-down boats and stoplights run their cycle in solitude. The inn at the corner has a square of cardboard firmly tacked over the "No" in NO VACANCY. In Rehoboth, the cottages were closed and shuttered and had an air of conspiratorial silence about them, a forlorn secrecy, as though a crime had taken place there.

From a poplar behind one cottage came the electric screech of a parrot, which erupted into a raucous debate, a chattering and whooping that traded back and forth between the trees. Then silence, as if the birds had all run out of breath at once. Then more staccato shrieks as a gang of eight came whirling through the pines, dipping low as they flew. For the first time I saw color: a brilliant grassy green with flashes of dark blue on the wings and a bluish-green pointed tail, utterly exotic.

The continental United States has only two native parrots, the Carolina parakeet, which was hunted to extinction in the early 1900s, and the thick-billed parrot, which used to visit the mountains of southeastern Arizona in flocks of fifteen hundred or more, but today appears there in much smaller numbers. In addition, a number of vagrant species have found their way onto the continent, among them budgerigars from Australia, rose-ringed parakeets from Asia and Africa, and South American monk parakeets, *Myiopsitta monachus*. The latter have cropped up in pocket colonies around the country. A dozen pairs live in a constellation of nests on the north side of Silver Lake.

Despite its common name, the monk is not a parakeet like the budgerigars but a true parrot, a psittacine, tough and stocky, about a foot long, with the thickset, barrel-necked look of a wrestler. Its eyes are beady black. Its beak is broad, powerful, and hinged at the skull, which enables it to eat pine-seed on the halfshell the way a man eats an oyster. I've seen one on the ground only once. Its big feet made it awkward and it moved with a kind of slow, pigeon-toed teeter. Parrots are zygo-dactylous: they have feet with opposable toes, two in front and two in back, which cramps their stride but gives them a primate's dexterity and grip. On the wing, these birds coerce your attention as tenaciously as a salesman with his foot in the door.

The monk parakeet is a native of central Argentina, a resident of the open forest, savanna palm groves, and pampas of the Argentine lowlands, which begs the question: What are these birds doing in Delaware? One story goes that a dozen monks destined for the pet trade escaped when their crate broke open at New York's Kennedy Airport in the 1960s and that our monks descend from these adventurous few. More likely, they're the offspring of escapees from pet owners and aviaries. While monks don't have the verbal abilities of some parrots (they can imitate whistles but are relatively poor talkers with little repertoire), and while their cackling chatter has none of that cheerful ring that people admire in caged birds ("possibly," says naturalist William Henry Hudson, "because it produces the idea in the listener's mind that the songster is glad to be a prisoner"), they are still popular pets in this country. In the late sixties, something like twelve thousand birds a year were imported to the United States. Those that escaped adapted to their new nation splendidly. In 1970, eight nests were found in the greater New York area. Three years later, the birds had colonized all five boroughs. Others had penetrated north to Plattsburg near the Canadian border and south into Maryland. Those that reached Delaware apparently found Rehoboth the equivalent of Mar del Plata. They have built three huge stick nests in the loblolly pines and have been reproducing ever since. They're lickerish eaters, who will happily consume cheese, suet, bread, and commercial wild bird seed to flesh out their usual diet of pine and sunflower seeds, grasses and corn. Their numbers are up by one or two a year. A rowdy, impudent lot, they seem utterly at home peacocking against the dark pines and sandy soil.

Monks are not the only immigrants here. The exotic is everywhere: mute swans nesting at the cape, those long-necked beauties brought to North America from Europe in the late nineteenth century to grace family estates; ring-necked pheasants from Asia foraging in our cornfields; English house sparrows nesting in our bluebird boxes; and European starlings everywhere, in great muscular black bands. The starlings were imported to this country to fulfill the zany dreams of a wealthy New York drug manufacturer who hoped to establish in his homeland every species mentioned by William Shakespeare. On March 6, 1890, he released eighty birds in Central Park in New York City. Now two hundred million starlings make their home in this country. That's three starlings for every house cat. Two or three times a day, the hackberry outside my study window fills with a fury of starlings out to ravage the sweet dark berries. At the first sharp sound they fly up, hundreds as one, and settle again the next tree over.

When the Swedish botanist Peter Kalm toured New Jersey in 1750, he found most of the European weeds already well established there. Thomas Nuttall's observations on Lewes include notes of a curious wanderer from the subtropics, *Proboscidea louisianica*, also known as cuckold's horns for the singular form of its large fruit. Today the fields around the town that have been plowed but not planted quickly sprout crabgrass, common mullein, and daisy fleabane, horseweed and Queen Anne's lace. Not one of these plants grew here before the Puritans landed. Most are natives of Europe and Asia. Even my yard is a thicket of exotic life, sown with immigrant grasses. By virtue of neglect I have a lawn that is roughly eighty percent crabgrass, mixed with rosettes of winter annuals such as fleabane and punctuated by the dents-de-lion, or lion's tooth, the common dandelion, a waif from Asia that came to the New World by way of Europe and now reaches down to the Patagonian steppes.

Edging the road along the Lewes canal is a vine with a lasso of perfume, a cloying, sweet summer scent that for me is a key to a set of memories having more to do with deciduous woods than white sand and blue water. I remember plucking the tubular flowers from thick tentacles of Japanese honeysuckle covering a fence near my childhood home. Here the vine covers cedars and fences alike. I have seen wild black cherry saplings strangled in its hold. A vigorous, twining climber, *Lonicera japonica* came from Asia in the 1860s, around the time Lewes first blossomed as a seaside resort. Since then it has become the botanical equivalent of *Rattus norvegicus*, traveling by runner and seed over thousands of acres of woodlands on the Eastern seaboard from New Jersey southward. At the cape it has become a kind of Japanese doppelgänger to the coral honeysuckle that Nuttall sought in vain.

Nearly everywhere on the cape foreign life grips. The dusty miller that ventures down to the high-tide line, where it thrives despite exposure to a stiff salt breeze, is a Japanese ornamental that escaped domestic bondage and now assumes a prominent post on dry sandy dunes from Quebec to Virginia. Bordering the roads are dense stands of multiflora rose, another Asian ornamental, a thick, hardy, prickly plant, robust in bloom, introduced sometime before 1811. In the early 1900s government officials believed it a botanical panacea, a living fence that would combat erosion, border highways, and contain livestock. So ballyhooed, it spread from coast to coast and is now considered a terrible weed.

In April and May, wisteria vines heavy with fat, pendulous racemes of lavender blossoms strangle the ruins of an old quarantine station on the cape. In the late 1880s the cluster of buildings—hospital, disinfecting house, crematory—saw a stream of immigrants subjected to tests for cholera, typhus, smallpox, and other contagious diseases. The vine came here a little earlier in the century by way of Philipp Franz Balthasar von Siebold, a Bavarian physician-botanist who lived for a time in Japan. He performed the first cataract operations there and wrote the definitive *Flora Japonica*. When he returned to his native country, he brought home more than a little of the Orient. It is said that he could be seen walking the streets of Leiden in a traditional Japanese kimono, tall, stooped, like some exotic crane. His beautiful wisteria found its way from gardens in Europe to gardens here, and now chokes our native oaks and cedars.

While Victorian plant collectors bear the blame for many botanical transplants, most uninvited ecological guests arrived with the first settlers in the soil and stone used for ballast on ships bound for the ports and harbors of the New World. The ballast was loaded into a ship's hold at the home port to provide proper balance and stability. Once a ship anchored at its destination, the ballast was dumped ashore with its weedy

Wisteria on trail at Cape Henlopen

cargo. Each dumping site became a little Ellis Island for crabgrass, dandelion, bindweed, literally thousands of immigrant species. (If you doubt the biological carrying capacity of dirt, consider this: Some years ago, when a small ball of earth was broken up and watered after three years in storage, it yielded eighty-two plants.) From coastal sites, these waifs hung on by ingenious devices—hooks, scales, spines, bristles, queer Lilliputian arrows and darts that bristle and grip—and spread by the sweat of others, by wool of sheep and hair of goat, by boot and hoof, by boat, wheel, bag, and gut. Most were adaptable and resilient, able to tolerate a wide range of physical conditions and partial to disturbed environments. They flourished wherever human activity had bared the soil.

These immigrants did not flow out into their new world

single file like cows in a gully, but leaked, percolated, infiltrated. As a result, native and foreign do not separate at some crisp blue line; they blur and dissolve, like the mixing of salt and freshwater, so that everything exists together in a new weave. This complicates the task of getting to know a place. I am more familiar with the corded twining of the honeysuckle stem than I am with the greenbriar vine that has grown here as a native for thousands of years. I can easily spot a Canada thistle, can recognize the silver fronds of dusty miller from fifty feet, but still have trouble distinguishing my wax myrtles from my bayberries, my marsh elders from my groundsel trees.

The ships that ferried vegetation from Lewes, England, to Lewes, Delaware, from Leipzig, Germany, to its New World sister, also carried animal stowaways. In the seventeenth, eighteenth, and nineteenth centuries, ships often sat in port for weeks or months before departing, time enough to grow a luxuriant colony of marine life on their hulls, says marine biologist James T. Carlton—seaweeds, sponges, barnacles, mussels, and sea anemones, clinging tight with threads and stalks. These communities sometimes grew three feet thick, creating a happy berth for fish, shrimp, and crabs.

And that was only the outer baggage. Just as there is honor among thieves, Aldo Leopold once said, so there is solidarity and cooperation among plant and animal pests. Inside the ship's hull, the burrows of shipworms and gribbles provided safe passage for other errant organisms. Shipworms are not worms at all but expert mollusks: They just look wormlike, with long, soft, tubular bodies. At one end are two small shells lined with rows of sharp-toothed ridges, which the shipworm uses to rasp away at wood, enlarging its burrows from the inside out. Known as the termite of the sea, it relies on wood for its livelihood. "This absolute dependence of a sea creature on something derived from the continents seems strange and incongruous," writes Rachel Carson. "Their numbers all over the earth must have been small until, scant thousands of years ago, men began to send wooden vessels across the sea." Then, for seagoing peoples everywhere, the shipworm became a scourge. On his third voyage to the West Indies, Christopher Columbus lost a vessel to these vermiform mollusks.

The shipworm's partner in crime is the gribble. These tiny isopods burrow from the outside in, feeding with their strong jaws, not on wood itself, but on a wood-dwelling fungus. I've seen pilings and driftwood along the shore peppered with their tiny holes. They can reduce wood to a spongy consistency and transform sound hulls into oceangoing habitats for other organisms.

When a ship made port with its marine masses huddled on its hull or snug inside its honeycombed interior, it sat at anchor while the immigrants fed, grew, reproduced, and then dispatched their offspring. Most of these transplants died. Success required the lucky meeting of a constellation of factors: good water quality, the right amount of salt, proper temperature, the right time of year, and good neighbors, preferably with few predators or competitors among them. The new arrivals had to be good at making do. Of those that gained a toehold, some, like the European marsh snail, settled into their new habitat benignly. I've found this snail, a demure quarter-inch gastropod that probably arrived on this coast on ballast stones sometime before 1840, nestled in marsh grasses near high-tide line and, occasionally, beneath rotting boards along the shore. It leads a life of flawless modesty, neither displacing native species nor significantly changing the community in which it settled.

The common periwinkle is another story. Populations of *Littorina littorea* lived on Canada's far northeast coasts thousands of years ago, but for some reason died out well before Columbus's arrival. They were introduced to Nova Scotia from western Europe in the early nineteenth century, either by accident with ballast rocks or deliberately for food (they're edible after light boiling in seawater). Now they dominate rocky shore habitats along much of the northern coast and reach into marshes and mud flats as far south as Maryland, where they're reduced in size a bit in translation from colder waters. In the mid-intertidal zone, they're the worst sort of guests, voracious omnivores with a habit of vacuuming up local seaweed communities, as well as the eggs of small invertebrates, thereby displacing other gastropods, eating them out of house and home. On our stretch of coast, periwinkles consume large helpings of the eggs of our native mud snail, *Ilyanassa obsoleta.*

The immigrant traffic has been two-way, of course. *Ilyanassa* has wound up in the San Francisco Bay, where it is reproducing furiously, fed by diatoms, bacteria, worms, and the egg capsules of the bay's native snail, whose place it is threatening to usurp. Our marsh grass, *Spartina alterniflora*, which traveled to England in the nineteenth century by seed in shipping ballast, has hybridized with its European counterpart to produce a new species wonderfully adapted to life on British mud flats; its vast, dense swards have changed the face of Britain's intertidal salt marshes. In Holland, our wild black cherry is a terrible pest; in Japan, the scourge is goldenrod.

Now that ships carry ballast of water rather than solids, in tanks that are bigger, cleaner, and more hospitable, the pace of these ecological swaps has gained speed. Those giant cargo ships moving like gray ghosts in and out of the mouth of the bay hold millions of gallons of water that were sucked up from one harbor and will be pumped back out in some other port halfway around the world, inoculating it with a kaleidoscopic array of planktonic plants and animals. These ships are like floating biological islands, transporting whole assemblages of coastal fauna from one bay to another.

So the Black Sea has its common Atlantic comb jellyfish by the hundreds of millions of tons which, by consuming huge amounts of zooplankton, has virtually wiped out that sea's anchovies. In return, the Black Sea has given us the sticky, fecund little zebra mussel that clogs our lakes and rivers. Our marshes have their Asian tiger mosquitoes, carriers of the virus for encephalitis and dengue fever, which found their way into this country in shipments of used truck tires. Puget Sound has its Atlantic slippersnails, and Cape May its *Hemigrapsus sanguineus*, a little green crab that arrived from Japan in 1988. And these are only the things we see. Powerful may be the impact of microscopic organisms such as tardigrades, too tiny to be seen, too numerous to be counted. The result of this ecological logrolling is a kind of homogenization of estuaries around the world. What was bizarre has become normal and what was normal is now an oddity; the alien grows as though it were indigenous, and the indigenous disappears. "The strange and wonderful are too much with us," says poet Amy Clampitt, and we have only ourselves to blame.

Yesterday morning I walked down to the ocean for a breath of air. It was one of those summer days veiled by fog and drizzle.

From the shore I spotted a pod of sixteen bottlenose dolphins and strolled with them along the beach a little way. They seemed to accept human company, almost to seek it. From time to time they came so close to shore that I could easily have reached them in a short swim. This I yearned to do, but some fear of invading their element or scaring them off kept me from it. They breached and fell, breached and fell. Adult. Adult. Calf. Adult. Adult. Two calves. Adult. Just keeping time with them from a distance made me feel elated despite the gloom.

On the way home, a flatbed truck with a tarp-covered mound passed me, leaving a wake of foul air, the unmistakable stench of rotting flesh. From the park naturalist I learned that the stink derived from the decaying carcass of a twenty-seven-foot killer whale, brought down from the coast of Massachusetts for burial here at the cape. Across the dunes from the ruins of the old quarantine station is a large expanse of sand that serves as a cemetery for marine mammals whose remains are studied by scientists at the Smithsonian Institution. Two other whales were buried there this summer, a pilot whale struck by a West German boat and a right whale pretty well cut up in a hit-and-run incident with an anonymous ship.

Alongside the whales lie several of those bottlenose dolphins that perished in the great dieout of 1987 and 1988. During that period twelve hundred dead dolphins washed up on the shores between Florida and New Jersey. Scientists believe that ten times that number died—half the mid-Atlantic population; the other bodies were likely eaten by predators or carried out to sea by currents. No one knows what caused the deaths, although research suggested that environmental toxins or a poisonous plankton may have sabotaged the animals' immune systems. Evidence has turned up linking such mass fish kills with a "phantom" alga, a kind of dinoflagellate found in estuaries along the Eastern seaboard. It lurks on the bottom of bays in a state of suspended animation until it senses the presence of fish. Then it cracks out of its cyst, swims up, and releases a poison that kills fish by the millions. Just hours later it retreats into hiding.

If kind often figures mysteriously here, so does number. The ups and downs of some species are easily explained. The demise of certain native plants, for instance. Canby's dropwort, sensitive jointvetch, bog asphodel, boneset, and featherfoil all have been driven out of their local redoubts by habitat destruction and overzealous plant collectors. The abundance of quiet, trapped waters in our mosquito control impoundments has multiplied the muskrat population. By plenitude of crop and scarcity of predator, deer overrun our fields and marshes; in places no green grows beneath their reach.

Hunting and an increased appetite for open summer beach among the general populace have nearly done in the piping plover, a gentle, airy bird, pale as a ghost crab, with a flutelike call and a tendency toward self-sacrifice. To distract predators from its brood, the little bird feigns injury, throwing itself on the ground, drooping its flight feathers, creeping around with wings outstretched, even collapsing utterly. The piping plover almost disappeared at the hands of hunters in the 1800s, but rebounded after passage of the Migratory Bird Treaty Act of 1918. Despite elaborate conservation efforts, its numbers are again dwindling, largely because it lays its salt-and-pepper eggs in hollows in the sand on those same stretches of beach popular with sunbathers, and with foxes, skunks, and, especially, feral cats.

Lewes offers no hospitable niche for rodents, immigrant or native, on account of its large community of wild cats, most of which descend from pets abandoned by summer visitors. They are a resourceful lot, tough, agile, wary of humans, with the pride and independence of a jaguar. At night I often hear their childlike mewing or the screams and stridency of mating. On a Sunday night last spring, under cover of darkness, some wild cat or other slid furtively between humps of sand, sidled toward a stretch of beach recently roped off for nesting plover, and in a few quick bites, halved Delaware's population of that rare little bird with a plaintive whistle.

Other dips and peaks are less well understood. Each fall, around the middle of October, our quota of monarch butterflies shoots through the roof. You see one tigerlike bit of night-spotted orange in erratic flight, then another, and another, before it finally dawns on you that you're watching a migration. The butterflies are on their way south to Mexico. Having just crossed the large expanse of bay from Cape May, they land exhausted in a patch of sun, light pouring through their half-open, tattered wings. One year they were here in huge numbers, hanging from the beach plums in long orange garlands. The next year, there were none. When I called the butterfly counters across the bay at Cape May, they confirmed the observation. The previous year they had seen more than seven hundred butterflies moving past a point on the beach during a fifteen-minute period. This year they saw one. The normally crowded migration routes all along the East Coast were nearly empty; the numbers had dropped by 90 percent. The leading expert on monarchs, Dr. Lincoln Brower, believed the decline had something to do with a devastating winter in the mountains of Mexico where the butterflies roost.

Snow geese were once hard to find here, but they made a comeback in the early 1980s; now they're everywhere in families of aunts and cousins. They start arriving from the north in early October in unravelling skeins, honking, circling, descending on our fields and marshes in great noisy flocks of thousands. In earlier years, they fed on the vast beds of eel-grass lining the Chesapeake and Delaware bays, but when these died out in the 1930s, they turned to our saltmarsh cord-grass. Voracious in appetite, they devour not just the grassy stalks but also the roots and rhizomes, damaging the plant's ability to regenerate. After a snow goose eat-out, the mud flats of our marshes look like they've been rototilled. Officials can't account for the bird's soaring numbers—though they believe the boom is somehow tied to weather patterns at its Arctic breeding grounds—so they've simply thrown up their hands and lengthened the hunting season. Even that tactic failed last year. Because of a poor nesting season, most of the geese that wintered here were older birds, wise to the ways of shotguns and counterfeit decoys. Out of flocks of tens of thousands, the total kill came to seventy-six birds.

One hot summer day I went trawling for samples of marine life on a research vessel from the University of Delaware. The trip offered the additional enticement of seeing whales. Heading out to open sea, I imagined multitudes of whales, not a lone finback or two, but animals broad on both bows, Ishmael's great Armada rolling softly on the surface. Before the arrival of European settlers, right whales abounded along this coast and in the bay. In the 1630s a Dutch merchant found great gams of whales in the mouth of the estuary and individual animals as far as six or seven miles upriver. But the blubber in the huge hanging lower lip of the right whale, Melville's "giant pout," yielded hundreds of gallons of oil, making it the "right" whale to hunt. By the early 1700s, the whales were all but gone from this coast; only a wandering few remain.

We saw none on our expedition. Our trawl dragged along the bottom at a depth of seventy feet. The first haul brought up a whelk, some crabs, a squid, a lion's-mane jellyfish, and one deer-nosed skate. In the days of the Dutch, nets brought up enough fish to feed thirty men. Our second haul yielded a single weakfish. It was beautiful to see—dark olive back peppered with black spots, lavender blue-green and gold on its sides, belly silver white and iridescent. It was a composition in color, as elegant as any peacock. The fish has a reputation as a fairly good fighter; its name comes from the fragile flesh in its mouth, which a set hook will easily tear. It shows up here in April, but not in the numbers it once did, thanks to the modern method of harvesting—high-speed pelagic trawls, which began in these waters in 1975. In 1980, the Atlantic coast catch exceeded 80 million pounds. Ten years later it was a fifth that.

It's the same with other fish: flounder, puffers, striped bass. Croakers were once so abundant in these waters that you could swamp your boat with a catch. Now they're rare. Even those flat, oily, inedible fish known as menhaden, whose giant schools of hundreds of thousands once turned giant pools of sea dull red or purple, have dwindled in number. A lowly, humble native, menhaden has also been baptized pogy, bughead, fatback, hardhead, silversides, pilcher, and mossbunker by the Dutch. The Indians called it "munnohquohteau," or "that which restores the earth," and taught colonists to place a fish in each hill of corn. For centuries thereafter, farmers used bunkers in one form or another to dress their acres.

At first the fish were caught with seines cast from twenty-foot skiffs. But with the advent of steamers and purse seines, a new commercial industry was underway. In the 1950s Lewes was the queen of menhaden fishing ports, home base for twenty-five giant boats, the "bony boats" or bunker steamers that sailed in summer from the company docks of Fish Products and Consolidated Fisheries carrying thirty-six-foot purse boats and seines twenty-five hundred feet long and thirty-six feet deep. Once a spotter plane tracked down the shoals, the crews set the seines from the sterns of two circling purse boats; when the boats met and passed each other, they pursed the catch, closing the net around twenty-plus tons of menhaden. In 1953 Lewes landed four hundred million pounds of fish, more than any other port in the country. Menhaden made up ninety percent of the catch. This bountiful state of affairs lasted for a few years, then deteriorated. In 1966 the industry ceased, dead of success.

Allowable catches for menhaden, croakers, herring, virtually all fish, are determined by a concept wildlife biologists call the maximum sustainable yield, which, in turn, is based on the notion of carrying capacity. The principle is this: In a caged population of fruit flies fed the same amount of food no matter what the numbers, a pattern will emerge. A few flies well-fed will reproduce rapidly. But when flies outrun food supply, deaths will rise to equal births, and the population will arrive at a balance, its carrying capacity. The idea is expressed with a mathematical equation that generates a growth curve shaped like an S. Smack in the center of the letter lies the point of maximum sustainable yield: A population of animals grows fastest when it's kept at half its carrying capacity.

There's a catch, though. The S-curve logic holds only for animals bred in laboratories under controlled conditions, not for animals in the wild. It fails to account for changes in the

Monarch butterflies on seaside goldenrod

environment—swings in temperature and food supply, fire, storms, disease, the ups and downs and ins and outs of other species, including humans, who, through our appetite for space and our chessplay with other species, are a source of ecological disturbance on the order of flood and fire, keeping nature in a perpetual state of uproar. Nor does it consider the mercurial behavior of individuals: a parrot with a sweet tooth, a goose who knows guns, a cat with a taste for plover.

We tend to favor the notion that nature exists in a state of balance or equilibrium in which plants and animals keep their own numbers pruned and in proportion. As if life were bent on consistency and selected for preserving the status quo. It's in our nature to see order, and when we don't see it, to try to impose it. We have to put things through our minds to make sense of them, and our minds crave pattern and order. So maybe what we glimpse is only what we desire, and the real constant is turmoil. Or perhaps there *is* a pattern there, a giant snaky curve of umpteen S's that represents a kind of floating equilibrium and takes into account all variables. It's just on a scale too big for us to see. A better model might be pi, that fantastic number that looks random but in fact may contain a design so vast and subtle it eludes our understanding. Perhaps beneath the surface busyness of fluctuating populations, the rattle and flash, there's a larger order, vague and monstrous like pi, tidal in its movement, and measurable only at the edges.

Seeds

of

Mischief

In the spring of 1631, near what is now the town of
Lewes, a crowd of Great Siconese Indians watched as a
small Dutch ship rounded Cape Henlopen and entered the
mouth of a small creek along the shore of the bay. Twenty-
eight white men disembarked from the Walvis and brought
ashore its cargo of lime, bricks, tiles, ammunition, tools, four
horses, twelve cows with calf, and several small whaling
boats. A few years before, reports had reached Holland that
"the savages of those quarters wear on their heads mostly
small feathers made of whalebone," and that great schools of
whales came so near to shore that harpooners could see them
from the beach and set off quickly for the kill. It was a good
spot. Dutch merchants had bought it from the Indians for
cloth, axes, beads, and other goods and named it Zwaanendael. To the west were marshes full of wildfowl, streams full
of fish, turtles, and muskrats, and thick forests of oak, wal-
nut, hickory, and pine, which the Dutch could smell far out
to sea. The colonists built a large house of yellow Holland
brick and a cookhouse to hold vats for boiling the whale
blubber; then surrounded the settlement with a wooden pal-
isade. A year later a Dutch merchant visiting the site found

the fort burned to the ground and the skulls and bones of animals and men scattered about. According to an account given by a Siconese man, the massacre by his people had resulted from a dispute over a piece of tin bearing the Dutch coat of arms.

Some days, by a queer coincidence of climatological circumstances having to do with warm ocean water and cold northerly air, a thick sea fog will stall on the edge of our coast, hang there like a shroud just along the littoral, while inland a quarter of a mile the sun shines brightly.

On such a day I walked a circuitous route at the cape that took me in and out of the fog. My path skirted the shore at first, then headed out to a spot southwest of the cape, a place where the past and the present come together like the clap of hands. It is a spur of woodland that points like a bony finger into the Lewes Creek Marsh. This piney ridge was once a curved sand spit on the old cape's bayshore; the prairielike marsh now surrounding it was a shallow lagoon. Over millennia, currents and rising sea level have shaped and reshaped this land. Out near the tip of the ridge are middens several feet deep containing pottery, arrowheads, bones, and piles of shells left by Native Americans twenty-five hundred years ago when they set up seasonal camp here to collect clams and oysters from the lagoon. The shells they discarded by the hundreds of thousands protected the spit from erosion and allowed a forest to grow.

Now the ground is soft with the needles of loblolly and pitch pine, and greenbriar grows in dense, impenetrable thickets. Littering the sandy soil are the curled black husks of earthstars, a mushroom with a tough inner sac that splits open during rain or fog to release thousands of minute spores. Holly

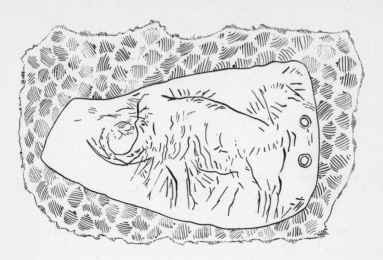

Holly Oak pendant

and young sassafras trees grow atop the middens. The people who built these trash heaps were only the last in a long line of indigenous peoples that called this coast home. Just how long a line has been the subject of heated debate.

Nested in a specimen drawer at the National Museum of Natural History in Washington, D.C., is a marine whelk shell of the species *Busycon sinistrum*. The shell is carved into a gorget, drilled with two holes, and engraved with the startling likeness of a mammoth. Known as the Holly Oak pendant, it came to light in 1890 when Hilborne T. Cresson, a field assistant with the Peabody Museum at Harvard, showed it to the Boston Society of Natural History. Cresson claimed that he had found the shell twenty-six years earlier, at the age of sixteen, while digging with his French tutor in Pleistocene deposits near the Holly Oak railroad station in northern Delaware. The Holly Oak pendant was touted as remarkable evidence that early man coexisted with extinct mammals, right here in the Delaware Valley, close to Cresson's birthplace, tens of thousands of years ago.

The shell was remarkable, too, for its close resemblance to another engraving of a woolly mammoth, this one incised on a fragment of a mammoth tusk discovered by scientists excavating at La Madeleine rock shelter in southern France the same year Cresson claimed to have made his find. Cresson's contemporaries noted the coincidence and dismissed the shell as a hoax, one of many plaguing an era obsessed with the search for evidence of early humans in the Americas. In 1891 Cresson was fired by the Peabody for stealing artifacts from an archaeological site in Ohio. Three years later he shot himself in a park in New York City. His suicide note revealed his fear that he was suspected of counterfeiting (money, not shell pendants), and that Secret Service detectives were continually on his track.

The Holly Oak pendant was forgotten for more than three-quarters of a century until it turned up again in the spring of 1976 in a larger-than-life-size image on the cover of the journal *Science*. Two Delaware scientists had rediscovered the pendant in the collection of the Smithsonian Institution in Washington, D. C., but had not gotten wind of its sordid past. They speculated that the engraving dated either from the Holocene epoch, 8000 to 4000 B.C., or from early Wisconsin and late Sangamon times, sixty thousand to one hundred thousand years ago. A few years later, a team of scientists from the Smithsonian proved the pendant a fake; radiocarbon dating placed the shell at less than a thousand years old, contemporaneous with other artifacts found at the Ohio site where Cresson lost his job as a Harvard field assistant. They also found the drawing of the tusk from La Madeleine that Cresson probably copied. Still, the Delaware scientists are unconvinced, refusing to give up the dream of finding tangible remains of ancient man in their valley.

Other, less controversial evidence suggests that small bands of Paleo-Indian hunters moved into this region in search of big game around twelve thousand years ago. Archaeologists digging in the Delaware drainage basin have turned up fluted spear points like those used by the big-game hunters of the southwest at the end of the Wisconsin Ice Age fifteen thousand years ago. No sites have been found on this coast, however: A sea swelled by melting glaciers submerged the late glacial shoreline of the Atlantic, drowning evidence of campsites or burying them beneath sediments.

Twelve thousand years ago sea level was more than three hundred feet below where it stands today. There was no bay at all, but a deep, cold, rushing river that emptied into the Atlantic fourteen miles beyond the present coast. As the summers grew warmer and the ice to the north melted back, the sea rose rapidly, about six feet per century, and the shoreline retreated at rates of up to thirty feet a year. Meanwhile, the soil thawed, the growing season lengthened, and spruce trees spread into the open land, with devastating effect on mammoths, mastodons, and musk oxen. When these big grazers disappeared, the people turned to hunting smaller animals and gathering more plant foods. As the warming continued, spruce gave way to hemlock and pines, and then to oaks.

By three or four thousand years ago, the rate of sea rise had slowed enough to create a stable estuary that would support communities of shellfish. Given the advantage of abundant food, the culture of the Woodland Indians flourished. People came together in early spring in villages and stayed through summer and early fall to harvest food from the sea.

They used nets of plaited grass and built weirs of branches on the mud flats to capture fish on the falling tide. They gathered roots and tubers, as well as berries, and butternuts, walnuts, and hickory nuts. They caught turtles. In fall they dispersed to hunt ducks, geese, wild turkeys, pigeons, and deer. By around 800 B.C. they had developed pottery and started cultivating crops. They were intimate with the landscape, knowledgeable about the behavior of the rising sea, and flexible, moving their camps with the shoreward movement of the coast. They made mistakes, too, overhunted, developed slash-and-burn farming techniques that were harmful to the land and abetted erosion. But their numbers were small enough that the effects were not lasting.

By 600 B.C. they were holding elaborate funerals. Up the coast at South Bowers, Delaware, is the site of a prehistoric cemetery where the Woodland people buried their dead more than two thousand years ago. The state has built a great cavernous, hangarlike building over the cemetery and excavated the burials. Inside it is cool and dark. The skeletons lie exposed in bare pits, heads oriented to the northwest. The museum plaques saw that many of the dead were surrounded by large caches of artifacts that told something of the way they lived: tools of deer bones and exotic stones, including banded slate from Ohio, suggesting that they traded with people far to the west (which may explain how Cresson's marine whelk shell found its way to Ohio), rare left-handed whelk shells, fossil shark's teeth, headdresses and jewelry made from deer antlers.

Staring down at the bones in the cool silence, the bare facts on those plaques seem insubstantial, say nothing of what these people and their ancestors felt about the changes in their land, the flooding they endured, the drought, the dwindling of game. The last burial took place around 1200 A.D. Sometime thereafter, the Woodland Indians slipped through a fissure in time to emerge as a people calling themselves the Lenape, or ordinary people, a band of Algonkian-speaking Indians that included the Great Siconese.

I walk out of the pine forest toward the cape in clear yellow light, along a road bristling with weeds, past the site of an atmospheric monitoring station, an odd assemblage of buckets and gauges surrounded by a chain-link fence. Up over a hump of dunes and I strike dense mist. It rises from the sea like an exhalation, obliterating all points of reference. I feel my way along the edge of the sea in the vaporous gray. About fifty yards down the beach a clean white thing rears up from the invisible ground. I move closer and see that it's only the thighbone of a deer. I wonder if it was brought downshore by some scavenger bent on dining by the sea or whether it traveled a watery route from inland slaughter. Strange things do turn up here, washed ashore or dumped. One summer I joined a group of volunteers cleaning up a stretch of beach. We hauled in a motorcycle at Kitts Hummock, bowling pins at South Bowers, an accelerator pedal at Cape Henlopen and a muffler from Lewes Beach, three refrigerators, two stoves, an air conditioner, a water heater, a shower curtain, and a toilet seat: twelve thousand pounds of stuff in one day. It was satisfying to clear this cumulus of human debris from white sand, but the things I worry about most are hard to collect, the toxic wastes and pesticides percolating through the waters of the river and bay (at last count thirteen varieties), the oil slicking the cormorant's wings, and especially the airborne chemicals that are heating up the planet and refiguring our spectrum of light.

I have been reading an essay that E. B. White wrote

thirty-five years ago about the problems of pollution. He wrote from his apartment in Turtle Bay, a section of Manhattan that boasted the heaviest sootfall in town. He wrote, he said, from a perfect position. The year I moved to Lewes, the Environmental Protection Agency listed my county as one of the smoggiest areas in the nation, with ozone levels that far exceeded federal standards. Per square mile, it said, Delaware has the worst sulfur emissions of any state in the country. Our industries release more than two hundred million pounds of pollutants a year, a large amount for so small a state. The rain that falls on Cape Henlopen is as acid as tomato juice; in summer, it has the pH of vinegar. The yellow-gray haze that shrouds the nation east of the Mississippi robs my view, too, cutting visibility from ninety miles to fifteen. Delawareans are known to be among the least healthy people in the nation. The first state is first in breast cancer and eighth in chronic disease. This may have something to do with the choices we make in diet and behavior. But if, as it is said, there is a continuum between the health of the environment and the well-being of the people who live there, we canaries would seem to be saying that this is a troubled mine indeed.

In the gray gloom of cold fog, it's hard to imagine the searing power of the sun's rays. But marine biologists say that even through cloud cover ultraviolet rays can affect organisms well below the ocean surface. Especially vulnerable are phytoplankton, those bright spicules and motes streaming through these waters and over the drowned three-quarters of the globe. To perform their acts of chemistry, converting solar energy and minerals into food that succors all oceanic life, they must float close to the surface, where they're exposed to high doses of ultraviolet light. Over eons of evolution, phytoplankton, as well as the countless organisms that feed on them, have evolved protective sun-blocking pigments—green, brown, crimson, and electric blue—that absorb ultraviolet radiation and prevent it from damaging the cellular mechanisms essential to life. Exposure to ultraviolet light stimulates these organisms to make more pigment, thereby boosting their defenses and lending them their brilliant hues. But there are limits. Too much exposure will damage their genes and their ability to grow and reproduce. Because so much of the food web depends on phytoplankton, even a small change in their composition and abundance could revolutionize ocean life.

There's been a lot of talk around here lately about the local effects of global warming. Scientists say that unless a turn is taken, the mean temperature on the surface of the earth will rise several degrees before the end of the next century. Of course, climatological prediction is a fuzzy business. Because scientists have pretty good numbers on the output of greenhouse gases in the past, they thought they could calculate with some certainty the expected rise in temperature on land. But when they actually measured surface temperatures around the globe, they found that Earth has warmed by only half the expected amount. No one knows why for sure. The simplest explanation is that the missing heat has been absorbed by the ocean, which is something of a wild card in the global warming equation. So too are clouds, which may either increase heating by trapping gases or lessen it by keeping out the sun's warm rays. Sulfur haze and the smoke from burning tropical forests and grasslands may have the same effect, cooling the earth by reflecting sunlight. Even sunspots play into the picture. It's a Rube Goldberg affair.

Still, even conservative estimates put the rise at three to eight degrees Fahrenheit over the next hundred years, enough of an increase to melt polar ice caps and warm the waters of the ocean. Warm water takes up more space than cold water, so a warming, expanding ocean, swelled by melt from ice caps, would raise sea levels better than three feet. Delaware is the flattest state in the Northeast, with most of its land less than fifty feet above sea level. Even a few inches' rise in the ocean would carry saltwater far inland, threatening our coastal roads and highways, our septic systems, even our water supply. A salt front creeping upriver would invade aquifers for cities up the Delaware, affecting something like twenty million people (once saltwater enters an aquifer, it's nearly impossible to remove), and by raising salinity, would destroy fish spawning and nursery grounds in the estuary. A rising sea would drown marshes. Given sufficient time and space, marshes can migrate backwards, but most of ours are backed up by manmade barriers they can't climb. The loss of wetland habitat would mean trouble for waterfowl, mammals, fish, and invertebrates.

When the fog lifts a little, it's not so oppressive, though the dunes and sea are still bleached of curve and colored only with soft, subtle moth hues. Gulls emerge ice-white and giant from the gray. I bend, pick up a stone, and skip it over the sea water. It clicks once, then sinks into silence. God asked Job: "Who can tilt the waterskins of the heavens?" This edge reminds me of the whole. An arrow's route across the ocean basin lie the Azores and the coast of Europe. This stretch of beach is tied to a community of coasts: Bangladesh, the low countries of Europe, the Maldives, the Nile Delta, the Bight of Bangkok, and Botany Bay, all threatened by the rising tide.

Sometimes, sitting out here on the beach at the tip of the cape or upcoast at the site of Zwaanendael, I imagine what it must have been like for the Great Siconese to see the ships of the

Dutch come into view. The European settlers came from old cultivated country to thick woods. They immediately set out to remake the new world in the image of the old. First to go were the forests of white oak, bald cypresses, and white cedars, good for barrelmaking, ship timbers, shingles, and boards. All land not needed for food was given over to tobacco, or "sotweed," which was in great demand in Europe. Because the crop exhausted the soil, the settlers cleared acre after acre of fresh land by burning forest, which required less labor than rotating crops or husbanding soil. "The aim of the farmers in this Country," wrote George Washington, "(if they can be called farmers) is not to make the most they can from the land, which is . . . cheap, but the most of the labour, which is dear, the consequence of which has been much ground . . . *scratched* over and none cultivated or improved as it ought to have been." Later the farmers would enrich the soil by mining the ancient middens for lime and collecting horseshoe crabs by the thousands each May to grind to meal and scatter over their fields. But for decades they just hacked down more forest. Runoff from the cleared land swept silt into the Delaware and its tributaries, radically changing the character of the estuary. The avalanche of sediment forced out such bottom-dwelling creatures as flounder and encouraged the growth and spread of free-floating plankton and wide-ranging fish.

Meanwhile the Siconese population had shrunk to vestiges from warfare and disease, especially smallpox. Loss of land forced some survivors to join other Lenape migrants as they moved to Pennsylvania and Ohio. In 1726, Reverend William Becket reported from Lewes on the composition of people living in his parish: "We have but few Indians & these seem obstinate to the means of conversion."

By the first decades of the eighteenth century, settlers had abandoned many of their fields to invading broomsedge and turned them over to grazing. They raised chickens, hogs, sheep, horses, and cattle. The sheep and cattle they turned loose in the high salt marshes to graze on saltmeadow hay. The hogs they set free in the woods, where they fouled the streams and damaged the soil.

The sheep and hogs didn't pay off. The cattle succumbed to anthrax, which arrived on these shores in a shipment of leather hides in the 1890s and spread rapidly. The chickens endured. Now those long, low chicken houses, processing plants, and feather-scattering transport trucks are everywhere, patrolled by huge morose flocks of turkey vultures. Farms are given over to endless rows of corn and soybeans grown mainly for chicken feed. Even this kind of homogenous farming is petering out these days. As I write, bulldozers at the site of the old fish-fertilizer plant near the cape are flattening the storage tanks that once held millions of gallons of liquid fertilizer used for farm fields around here. The owner threw over his old business in favor of residential development. "We took a long look at the region," he said, "and saw that this area's going to be growing more people than crops." In recent years, my county has lost more than five thousand acres of farmland to development. Keep perfectly quiet and you can almost hear the sound of cement moving like a rising tide over the farm fields, creating a matrix for subdivisions, malls, roads, and parking lots.

The wizards of long time assure me that ruptures of the sky and climate are not new things under the sun. Stratospheric ozone has thinned out or disappeared altogether many times during the long history of the planet, allowing the sun to saturate life with ultraviolet radiation. Organisms have adapted. The same goes for swings in temperature. When life on Earth began, around three and a half billion years ago, our sun was a weak young thing, shining faint rays that could not possibly have kept the planet from freezing. Earth was saved from a frigid fate only by its lack of land and steady spinning. Water absorbs more sunlight than land, so the absence of big continents meant higher temperatures. The spinning kept weather systems small and bound to the equatorial regions, reducing the amount of cloud cover and allowing more warming sunlight to reach the planet's surface. Since that time, the sun has steadily increased its brightness, growing nearly 30 percent more luminous.

Changes in Earth's position relative to the sun and in the relationships between land and sea have caused more recent big wiggles in climate. In fact, say some scientists, temperature swings in the last few million years may have led to the evolution of our own species. In the shells of tiny ocean animals called foraminifera are preserved records of ancient climate shifts. Foraminifera retain more of a certain oxygen isotope from cool periods than from warm. Layers of these shells point to two pulses of global drying and cooling, one around five million years ago, and one a couple of million years later. The first cold, dry spell may have caused forests to give way to grasslands and open savanna, forcing a tree-dwelling quadruped ape to come down out of the branches and forage afar on two legs; the second may have led to emergence of the genus *Homo*.

Back at the salt marsh spur, I'm kneeling in a little grove of pin and southern oaks, species that fare well in poor, sandy soils. A

Shell midden on marsh finger

thousand years ago, a few seeds germinated in the bare sand on this spit, weedy species that held sway for a short time, but mulched the land, made it a little richer than when they found it, preparing the way for the disorderly, tangled thickets of vines and shrubs, the pines, hollies, and sapling oaks that now flourish.

On the edge of the spur, I catch sight of a rough-legged hawk hovering above the sea of grass-that-was-lagoon, all appetite and burning purpose. Out here in the sun again, what keeps grinding its way into my mind is this: The revolutions in climate and landscape that used to take thousands or millions of years may now occur in a match-snap of geologic time. Human activity threatens to make big changes in a century or less, too fast to allow much of life to evolve and adjust to new conditions. The species most likely to prosper in a rapidly warming world are the fleabanes and starlings of the world, those able to adapt to a wide range of environments. The losers will be rare species, those adapted to special niches or locked in relationships that depend on special circumstances of timing and weather.

Take migratory shorebirds. If the earth warms, chances are that the two critical timing signals for birds and insects— length of day and temperature—will uncouple. Day length, the signal that gets a shorebird up and out of Patagonia one evening in March, won't change, but temperatures will. Warmer days earlier in the year will cue plants and insects to start growing and reproducing earlier. So a migrating bird that arrives at its northern feeding and breeding grounds on schedule will miss the emergence of its prey. I wonder what will happen to red knots if the horseshoe crabs of Delaware Bay spawn in April instead of May.

As the earth warms, the climate will travel northward, scientists say, about thirty-five to fifty miles for each rise of one degree. With no time to adapt, plants and animals may have to leave their southern digs and pursue some more northerly niche. Local officials have begun to discuss the possibility of creating corridors, strips of natural habitat that will allow these refugees to funnel north, if necessary, bypassing human barriers. But there's no guarantee that the animals will use them. Recent studies on salamanders showed that a third of the creatures provided with these paths of green never found their way to them, but wandered into bare, inhospitable tracts and died there.

Much ocean life finds shelter in the shallow water of estuaries and coastal shelves, which heat up more quickly than deep ocean. Warmer temperatures affect the feeding, growth, and reproduction of many plants and animals. Those living in the brackish nirvana of estuaries may not tolerate the warm salty seas between their homes and some cooler northern estuary. How does one create corridors in the sea, cold and relatively salt-free?

Maybe the earth will warm eight degrees over the next century. Maybe not. Maybe the ocean will kick in, or sunspots, or haze, and the temperature will only rise a degree or so. Maybe it will take a hundred years to see a notable difference, or a thousand. The point is this: We have sown the seeds of mischief, changed the character of change.

I know that we are not the first species to alter the atmosphere. Two billion years ago photosynthesizing microbes began to break down water and expel oxygen as a byproduct. The oxygen killed most other organisms, but ultimately created an atmosphere that would support life. I know, too, that even if polar ice caps melt, glaciers shrink, ecosystems migrate, and seas rise, the earth will endure, whirling through space at a thousand miles per hour, and life, too, in some guise. But I am not calmed by this. My yardstick is the human yardstick, the holiness of everyday life, what I consider a legitimately parochial interest. When I think of what we are doing, have already done, to the world that is the matrix of our being, I feel a black wave of despair. Years ago when my mother was sick with cancer, she wrote, "The habit of mind that comes from years of preoccupation with managing unhappy situations is not easily broken." She was speaking in personal terms, but reading this years later, I wonder whether it doesn't apply to most of us.

Loren Eiseley once wrote about the death of the white whale in *Moby Dick*: "That great solitary beast . . . saw as it floundered in its death throes, two separate worlds. It saw with one dimming affectionate eye the ancient mother, the heaving expanse of the universal sea. With the other it glimpsed with indescribable foreboding the approaching shape of man, the messenger of death and change. So it was that the dying whale in its dissociated vision had arrived, if momently, at the one true place where the nature of the past mingles with the onrush of the future and is borne down forever into darkness."

I know that one picture of ourselves as agents of death, hurling harpoons at a wounded earth, scurrying toward suicide, making beautiful things disappear and turning the rest to lead, is only half the story. Immense curiosity and a filial love of life threaded in our genes is driving us in quite a different direction. Our activity, like our science, gives rise to truths as well as hoaxes. I only hope that we are stumbling, despite ourselves, on an erratic path toward a deeper understanding of nature and a more dignified, honorable relationship with it.

Spindrift

$\mathcal{T}$he sea has gone the color of pewter. A sharp, clean wind blows scuds of foam along the beach and forces my gaze downward; fine sand stings my legs. It is spring, a day or two after a violent storm. Near the waterline are scarps two feet high, miniature cliffs where the charged-up surf has gnawed its way into the continent. I have come down to the shore with my father, who is visiting for a day or two. We have brought binoculars in the hopes of spotting a storm waif, a petrel, perhaps, or a shearwater—some birds will fly for days before a storm at sea, then drop as soon as the storm hits land—but we see only Bible black grackles fighting the wind and a knot of three gulls hunkered down on the sand like clenched fists. The storm has resculpted the contours of the beach, scoured it of all familiar form. The beach grass is scribing arcs in the sand like dark circles under tired eyes.

The storm was born when a cold front moving in from the northwest collided with a mass of hot, muggy air from the south, prompting a line of violent thunderclouds. At the ferry dock, on the fishing piers, people dropped what they were doing, stood and watched the huge black curtain move across the water. Soon they were standing in freakish noon darkness as complete as a total eclipse of the sun, and in stillness, save for the steady tick and creak of boats on their moorings and the tide slip-slapping beneath the piers. The moment had that dreamlike quality of a luminist painting where time rolls forward. When the storm finally struck, rain lashed down, pelting the sand like buckshot. Winds gusting to eighty miles per hour fueled ten-foot seas that took the beach apart.

Our footsteps break the crust of the upper beach with the good crunch of dry sand, but as we head down toward the water, we slog along in the softer sediment, and my dad's breathing grows heavy. He has recently recovered from an allergic reaction that nearly killed him. During a routine diagnostic test, so small a wrench as iodine—an element in seawater, rocks, and soil, and in small amounts essential to our own well-being—produced an anaphylactic attack that unhinged his whole system, swelled his throat, shut his airways, made his heart stop cold. My father is an energetic man with a keen intellect, a good sense of humor, and passion for his work. He is careful in his habits and attentive to his health. But here was something utterly beyond control, a case of mistaken identity by his immune system, a small blunder that nearly cost his life.

When my stepmother, Gail, called in a shaken voice, I thought: *No. Not him. Not now.* By the time I reached the hospital, his heart had stabilized and the threat of death had passed. Gail and I stood by his bed in the critical care unit waiting for some sign of consciousness. Between us hung the deep unspoken fear of mental diminishment. When he finally stirred, he said in a voice muffled through tubes and masks. "My first sick day in twenty years."

As we round the cape, my father's chest is tense and heaving. For rest, we find a log thrown up by the sea and sit looking down at the little wrecks beaten by the surf: legless shells of lady crabs, mermaid purses torn from their moorings, the busted-up helmets of horseshoe crabs.

The last hurricane-force storm to hit this region was a giant northeaster that struck hard on Ash Wednesday, 1962. The U.S. Weather Bureau called it an extratropical cyclone, "unusual in composition and behavior." It was a saucer-shaped affair, a strong circular low-pressure system reaching up to forty thousand feet that moved out of the Midwest the first weekend in March, crossed the Appalachians, dumping three feet of snow in Virginia, and then traveled east toward the coast. Monday night it joined another, uncharted storm developing in the Atlantic, forming a giant trough of low-pressure air from Cape Hatteras to Cape Cod, six hundred miles long and three hundred miles wide. Winds blowing down the long fetch of that trough whipped up twenty- and thirty-foot waves that crashed down on the coast.

All day Tuesday, the rain fell and the waves came closer and closer upon each other, slamming into the shore every six or seven seconds. With the new moon of Ash Wednesday came heavy tides, five to ten feet above normal, which sent the sea sliding far up into the bay, into salt creeks and marshes. In Lewes, the swollen bay cut straight through the beach and moved in to meet the canal, carrying with it porches, roofs, and trailers. Up the coast at Bowers Beach, the high tide pushed houses off their foundations and ferried them a mile or more back into the marshland. Downcoast, the sea dredged new channels through the barrier beaches and reduced boardwalks, houses, and hotels to rubble.

At daybreak on Thursday, people emerged from shelters to survey the damage. They moved about numbly in the dull, sodden morning, stopping and standing before front doors banked by mountains of sand, cars submerged in seawater, boats torn loose from their moorings and splattered against pilings. In Bethany, Rehoboth, and Ocean City, five or six feet of sand packed Route 1 and some of the lower streets, topped by chairs, cocktail tables, books, kitchen utensils, and hotel beds still perfectly made. Off Lewes Beach an eight-room house unfamiliar to townspeople rose and fell in the surf. At final count, the storm left sixteen hundred people injured and twenty-five dead. It was the storm of the century, the sort that drives home the foolhardiness of getting mixed up with the coast on anything like a permanent basis.

I pick up a tiny seastar on my finger, an apparent casualty of the recent storm, but it soon curls one arm, and I set it down in the damp sand near the surf. A grackle straddles an overturned horseshoe crab, cocking its head upside down to get at the meat. Another one plucks a rolling mole crab from a retreating wave; there's a quick flash of orange innards before the bird swallows. The day my father left the hospital he found that everything he touched and smelled gave him intense pleasure, even simple things, like the smell of the earth before rain. The experience had the effect of a kind of scouring, a sloughing off of layers. It made him look at things he had been running past for years, made him rethink life and vow to savor what remains. That meant focusing less on what is considered productive in the narrow sense and more on the ordinary, the everydayness of life. It meant more time with Gail, more bird-watching, and more Bach. Also, more lovingness.

This wind could drive a straw into a tree. My dad's hat blows off and skips toward the surf. I run after it, miss it on the

Wrack line after spring storm

first grab, and plunge into the waves to retrieve it, soaking my sneakers. It took me a long time to forgive my father's leaving; it is only in recent years that I have come to know him well. The love I felt for my mother was a kind of blurring of boundaries; her death came close to self-erasure. Looking up at my father over the chiseled beach, I realize that I love him not only as a child loves a parent, but as a good companion in this shifting world. I want to see him finish out his odyssey, see the wisdom of his later years. He stands to take the water-soaked hat, still breathing heavily. He hugs me tight, and I feel like leaping in a frenzy of feeling, of urgent love. Instead I lean in and together we set our shoulders against the wind and go the short way home.

* * *

When my husband and I came to Lewes three years ago, it was with the hope of having a child and giving it an early dose of salt air and warm sand. But nature at first didn't cooperate. Now it's time to leave here, move inland to the mountains, knowing that the first outdoor smells of this baby finally growing inside me will not be the sweet stink of mud flats but some waft of woodsy soil or meadow clover, the smells I grew up on.

This place has taught me: If there is some design in this world, it is composed equally of accident and order, of error and deep creativity, which is what makes life at once so splendid and so strange. I have been able to see this more easily along the littoral, where the meetings and transitions are everywhere apparent.

"It gives one a feeling of confidence to see nature still busy with experiments, still dynamic, and not through or satisfied because a Devonian fish managed to end as a two-legged character with a straw hat," Loren Eiseley once wrote. "There are other things brewing and growing in the oceanic vat . . . things down there still coming ashore." I learned recently that marine biologists exploring the continental slope a few miles off Cape Henlopen and Cape May made an astonishing discovery. In the cold, the dark, the density at the bottom of the sea, a zone once thought utterly lifeless, they found an amazing array of creatures. From an area of soft ooze roughly the size of two tennis courts, they pulled 90,677 animals (not counting the little things, the nematodes, copepods, ostracods, and other meiofauna). In the group were representatives of 171 families and 14 different phyla (land has only 11 phyla). Each of the more than two hundred samples brought up something different: jellyfish, anemones, corals, snails, clams, peanut worms, ribbon worms, beard worms, and lamp shells—bivalved creatures that look like mollusks but are in fact brachiopods, animals of deep antiquity. Of the 798 species, 460 had never been seen before.

It seems that the life of the deep sea has diversified by distributing itself over countless little environments, many of them created by the animals themselves: mounds of sediments, depressions, empty worm burrows, patches of seaweed, glass sponges rising on graceful stems. Food drifts down to these seafloor habitats in erratic pulses—a decaying fishhead or the carcass of a seal—creating tiny local communities different from those just a few meters away. Scientists estimate that they've surveyed less than a tenth of one percent of the deep sea. Given the area of the seafloor, something like three hundred million square kilometers, this vast domain might hold a reservoir of ten million undescribed species. And not all of them small. Some giants lurking in the deep sea pastures have recently surfaced in human awareness: tube worms ten feet long with furry blood-red tentacles living around deep-sea vents, the giant squid *Architeuthis*, big as a city bus, which has never been seen but has yielded up a monstrous tentacle or two. News came this spring of the first new species of whale to be discovered in nearly three decades, an elusive beaked creature with a tiny cranium, a long jaw, few teeth, and an appetite for squid.

Imagine inventing water—two hydrogen atoms and a single oxygen atom in a V-shaped molecule with an odd electrical asymmetry that makes one molecule bond with another and thus holds the ocean together, along with salt and all the other earthly elements in seawater—and then on top of it a hammerhead shark, a sixty-foot squid, this whole rich broth of life!

That I should be surprised by the sea's diversity is a sign of deep land bias. After all, life was born in the sea, and evolution's big bang, that explosive radiation of animal forms in which nearly all the major groups now on earth first appeared, took place in primordial waters. Of these groups only a small number evolved the basic trick of living outside the ocean. Movement to land was the exception, not the rule.

The sea has a habit of upsetting expectations. Among my favorite new findings is one that has stood on its head the traditional view of ocean life as a linear or pyramidal food chain, in which plankton are eaten by tiny crustaceans such as copepods, which feed the larger animals, and so forth, in an uninterrupted line from smallest algae to largest whale. The idea goes back a long way. Peter Brueghel the Elder drew the first picture of it in 1556, a nightmarish image of an enormous glassy-eyed fish beached on a river bank, its gaping mouth regurgitating a cornucopia of smaller fish, which are in turn regurgitating even smaller fish. Some early species of marine pathologist is slicing open the belly of the big fish with an oversized bread knife, while his unfortunate partner stumbles away, half man, half fish, his piscine appetite apparently having gotten the better of him.

This pyramidal view held for centuries until those marine ecologists charged with the duty of finding ever smaller particles in the sea discovered picoplankton, bacteria less than two microns in size—hundreds of millions in every liter of seawater. These marine bacteria are too small to be eaten by the tiny crustaceans that are the major food source for much of the marine web. The bacteria feed on waste produced by algae and protozoa, and are, in turn, eaten by some of the same organisms.

Then came the discovery that in a single teaspoon of seawater there are more than seventy-five million viruses, those tiny particles composed of gene and protein that exist somewhere between the living and the dead. Viruses do not eat, move, or reproduce on their own. When they invade a living cell, they commandeer its genetic machinery and reproduce. The cell dies and its membrane bursts, releasing a flood of new virus particles, which go off by the thousands. (We are swimming in a sea of DNA.) The chief aim of these marine viruses, it turns out, is to infect their larger microbial brethren, the bacteria, and also phytoplankton. In so doing, they may determine the mix and abundance of those organisms that feed so much of marine life. Since a virus can destroy a whale as well as a bacterium, it's not at all clear what sits at the bottom of the pyramid or the top. In fact, the only certainty is that the marine food web is no pyramid at all, but an immense tangle of biological activity from surface to floor.

Among those hordes of viruses floating in the sea today are perhaps the descendants of some that moved into the earliest cells, carrying bits of foreign genetic information, wayward genes that eventually led to the whole multifarious tumult of life, including our own odd species, with its tendency to find more meaning in life on the other side of stopped breath.

Edward O. Wilson has said that the human mind does not have an instant capacity to grasp reality in its full chaotic richness, the accidents and quirks, the unruly elements, the organisms imperfect and emergent. The world abounds in phenomena that are still mysterious and unpredictable. What happens to a person in anaphylactic shock is well understood, but not the question of why the same allergen will produce body-wracking in one individual and no response in another. That is still a puzzle having to do with the question of genetic individuality. We have only a ghost of an idea of what triggers the differentiation of cells into a photosynthesizing cell in a strand of marsh grass, the sperm of an osprey, or the cell of a human heart. The full spectrum of life—its subtle relationships, strange couplings, chains of dependence, as evident on a mud flat as in a rain forest—remains unplumbed.

Weather, too, is a conundrum. We can restart a man's heart but we can't forecast the landfall of a hurricane. Some climate experts say that weather is simply a seamless web of abnormalities, affected by each gust of wind, each flap of a butterfly. And now it's apparent that things could be even more iffy than they are. Scientists studying the planets of our solar system have found that they tend to tilt chaotically on their axes. The accumulation of small gravitational tugs from neighboring planets, coupled with each planet's own wobbly rotations, sets up resonances, which change the shape of the planet's orbit and the tilt of its axis. A planet's tilt angle determines the seasons. Mars may undergo chaotic variations in its tilt angle of up to 85 degrees, causing wild extremes of climate. Fortunately for us, the moon, so big and so close, exerts enough gravitational pull not only to heave the oceans twice daily, but to keep Earth's tilt from varying more than a degree or two. So in a sense, the moon is our climate regulator, stabilizing us enough to permit our own familiar brand of chaotic weather and the evolution of life.

Given all the confusion and complexity in the world, so much at sixes and sevens, so much wild change and variety—given all this, the wonder is that there is order or structure at all, likenesses or rules, universals on a giant scale.

I never fully understood my father's love for mathematics until I read about pi, that transcendental number with its digits marching to infinity in a pattern as yet unfathomable. "Pi is obvious in the disks of the moon and the sun," writes Richard Preston. "The double helix of DNA revolves around pi. Pi hides in the rainbow, and sits in the pupil of the eye, and when a raindrop falls into water pi emerges in the spreading rings. Pi can be found in waves and ripples and spectra of all kinds, and therefore pi occurs in colors and music. Nature seems to know mathematics."

The shore has taught me this, too. Out on the tip of the cape one morning, cloudy gray but gleaming, I saw things the way physicists say they are, when a dense cloud of shorebirds appeared, then vanished, then appeared again like a flash of mercury, their swerves and dips and semaphore twists so unified they seemed a single wave rolling from light to dark to light again.

The evolutionary reason for flocking is defense; hawks seem confounded by the unity of the flock and are unable to concentrate their hunger on any one individual. A flock may rush an attacking raptor, bursting apart in its face. The phenomenon has been noted in fish, too. Minnows zip into a compact quiver when alarmed by the rising shadow of a predator, and perform complex maneuvers in the face of attack, splaying apart like a fountain, or exploding outward radially like a bursting bomb. The fish rely on their sense of distant touch, the lateral line, to "know" where their neighbors are. No collisions have ever been observed.

Flocking birds and schooling fish seem to have entered a dimension in which signals are superfluous. A zoologist who filmed a flock of thousands of dunlins discovered that the swerves and turns spread through a flock from bird to neighboring bird in a seventieth of a second. That's about three times faster than the speed at which a single bird can react to the movement of its neighbor. The high-speed patterns of motion in flocks and schools are so fluid, precise, and well coordinated that they have suggested to some scientists ideas of thought transference and electromagnetic communication. But the patterns more likely result from individual birds and fish following a few simple behavioral rules: Avoid predators, match the speed of your neighbors, and don't collide with them. The patterns unfold on their own, from the bottom up. Beautiful they are and yet, presumably, they depend upon no puppeteer, no "higher intelligence" at all.

Little examples abound of disorderly systems crystallizing into neat mathematical order. When waves encounter some random variation on the shoreline, even something so diminutive as a child's sandcastle, the water will reshape the anomaly by depositing sand or carrying it away until it has sculpted evenly spaced scallops along the beach. Drizzle sandgrains on a pile in a steady trickle, and the pile will grow into a cone-shaped mound with a characteristic slope or angle, the angle of repose, a convex version of the ant lion's pit. The pile will reach this state all by itself, without any hand shaping it. Add one more speck of sand to the pile, and it may cause just a tiny shift in a few grains or, if one collision leads to another in a chain reaction, a catastrophic landslide. Scientists note that little shifts are common; big ones, rare. The law dictating the frequency and size of the avalanches is ubiquitous in nature. It's seen in the flow of water through a river, the pattern of energy release during earthquakes and forest fires, the ebb and flow of sunspot activity, even the evolution of species.

It seems to me that the mind is peculiarly well equipped to find beauty in the unity among vastly different things, to take pleasure in the discovery that we are 70 percent water, like the planet, that the chemical composition of our blood is strangely similar to that of seawater. The more unlikely the likeness, the more beautiful.

Take chaos, the amplifying of small uncertainties in dy-

Close-up of wrack line

namic systems like water and weather and the oscillations of the heart, which results in behavior that cannot be predicted in the long term but follows mathematical laws nonetheless. Chaos is everywhere in the natural world. When blue mussels bunch together higgledy-piggledy in chaotic fashion on the sea bottom, the bumpy, irregular surface of the thicket causes turbulence in the water flow, a maelstrom of eddies and whorls still not fully understood. (There's so much going on in turbulent water flow that not even the world's fastest supercomputers can track a cubic centimeter of water for more than a few seconds.) It turns out that the chaotic flow draws phytoplankton from the surface down to the bottom dwellers, enhancing the mussels' food supply. So a mollusk finds chaos a part of its essential everyday equipment.

The same may be true for us. Some scientists are convinced that our minds spend much of their time in a state of chaos directly analogous to that of the weather or the turbulent flow of water over a bumpy bed of mussels, that it is the very property of the brain that makes perception possible. In response to the smallest of inputs, vast collections of neurons shift their pattern of activity, allowing the brain to respond flexibly to the outside world. As Wallace Stevens says: "The law of chaos is the law of ideas, of improvisations and seasons of belief."

When I return to the cape a week or so after the storm, the scarps are mostly gone, dissolved again into the beach face, but the ocean is still roiling with several days of wind and rain. On the way here, I saw two male summer tanagers razzing each other, staking out their spring territory, and a collection of kingbirds on the phone wires above the beach plum, which has erupted in full white bloom.

A light breeze is blowing as I head out along the ocean side toward the tip of the cape. Bits of spindrift blowing across the sand lodge and pass into iridescent bubbles. Last night I read about a new theory linking bubbles with the origin of life. It says that the simple chemicals present on early Earth— hydrogen, nitrogen, carbon—gave birth to such big complicated molecules as RNA, DNA, and proteins with the help of bubbles on the surface of primordial seas. The theory is the boldest kind of guesswork, but is rooted in some solid facts. Bubbles are just whiffs of gas enclosed in a skin of water, born of the action of wind and waves, the splash of raindrops and snowflakes, the belch of undersea volcanoes. At any given moment, they cover three or four percent of the ocean surface, an area roughly the size of North America. As a bubble travels through the atmosphere and ocean, it scavenges organic materials, minerals, metals, and clay particles, then concentrates them within its skin. Here they grow in size and complexity in response to changing temperatures and pressures. When the bubble pops, a rich little brew of chemicals is spit into the air and carried aloft by winds. The theory goes that sometime during Earth's first 700 million years, atmospheric chemistry triggered by lightning and ultraviolet light from the sun worked its alchemy on these chemical dollops, and the molecules grew even more complex, fell to sea as rain or snow, and were once again sucked into a bubble. The cycle was repeated again and again in the early seas, until some lucky collection of concentrated chemicals vaulted into being as a nucleic acid, parent of us all.

Sand has been moving during the night, riding currents from the south to feed the cape. My progress around the hook is slow. There's new ground here. It's low tide. And every few feet I stoop to scrutinize the wrack line, the beards of seaweed and smashed clam shells. I'm moving slowly these days, anyway, feeling heavier and more than a little morning sick. Pregnancy has made me first and foremost my physical self, a warm thumping habitat of bone and blood. I should be at home packing, not dawdling over sea grass and bubbles. But it's good to be out: schools of little whitecaps, cries of the sanderling and the osprey, light sea wind like a child's breath.

Acknowledgments

I am indebted to the Delaware State Arts Council for awarding me a year's fellowship, which helped finance the field work in which the foundations of this book were laid.

I am also deeply grateful to the many people who gave freely of their time and expertise.

A number of scientists and naturalists informed and instructed me, among them, James T. Carlton, Randall V. Cole, William Hall, Michael Kennedy, Evelyn M. Maurmeyer, William H. Meredith, Douglas C. Miller, J. P. Myers, Denise Seliskar, Paul Spitzer, Chester Stachecki, and William C. Sturtevant.

Bill Frech provided dozens of hours of companionship and patient tutorials for a beginning bird-watcher. Bill and Sally Fintel, too, shared with me their birding expertise, as well as that singular moment with a finback whale.

During the writing of the book, my neighbors in Lewes, Phillip Hatchell and Gonzalo Martinez, gave food, friendship, and perspective.

Linda Smith and John and Symmie Newhouse offered generous support and encouragement, as did Barbara and Herb Morton and Marjorie and Karl Ackerman.

Karin Grosz's artistic talent and broad knowledge of natural history combined to make the twenty beautiful illustrations that grace the book. They enhance it immeasurably.

Several friends and fellow writers read the manuscript in its various forms and made valuable suggestions: Donna Lucey, Barbara and Herb Morton, Bobbi Snow, Henry Wiencek, and Ann Zwinger. Ann's warm, wise letters kept me afloat throughout the project.

Melanie Jackson's enthusiastic response to the manuscript, her skill in finding it a good home, and her always sage counsel were much appreciated, as were Dawn Drzal's belief in the book and expert efficiency in shepherding it through the publishing maze. My debt to Richard Howorth of Square Books in Oxford, Mississippi, is great: at critical points he offered thoughtful advice and unstinting support.

It was Nan Graham who first saw the potential of the manuscript. To her, the angel at my table, I owe far more than I can say.

Finally, I'd like to give loving thanks to Gail and Bill Gorham for the gift of Lewes and for their understanding and deep generosity; and to my husband and fellow writer, Karl Ackerman, for his bedrock support and intelligent insights at every stage of the project.